The "3 Things"
That Make All the Difference:

Communicating More Effectively at Work & Home

Second Edition

Raymond L. Falcione, PhD

The "3 Things" That Make All the Difference:

Communicating More Effectively at Work & Home

Second Edition

Raymond L. Falcione, PhD

Dedication

To my Family

Dorcas, Ray & Krista, Joe & Charisa, Aaron & Sloane,
Anna, Laura, Olivia, Ray III
Savanna, Lily & young Aaron,
Kris & Tom, Lou, Tony & Pat,
Louis & Lydia

Acknowledgement

I'd also like to thank Rita Balenger, Antonette Chahine, Rosalind Cloud, DeeDee Collins, Sally Heisler, Lana Lyskin, Brian Malone, Jean Tisinger, and Jim Zoerkler for the support they have shown me throughout my career.

Table of Contents

Preface

Thank you for reading this second edition of the "3 Things". In this edition, much remains the same, but I've enhanced certain sections with new material and introduced a completely new chapter on Critical Thinking. I always felt I should have said more about certain subjects, so I decided to do this revision. Unfortunately, I still feel I should say more, but maybe that's for another time. The additional chapter on Critical Thinking may be controversial to some, but I thought it needed to be added to a book that purports to be about communication. I hope you find the additions useful.

Several years ago, I wrote a book entitled *The Guide to Better Communication in Government Service*. It focused on the distinction between government agencies and private sector organizations. The book emphasized that even though these organization types are different in terms of their goals, objectives, and function, many of the necessary communication skills had applications across those contexts. Since then, I have thought about rewriting the book to show that the skills focused on back then are certainly applicable today. They are applicable in private and public sector organizations, and in our homes and interpersonal relationships generally. I intend to expand on the case that these communication skills are relatively generic, and they have utility in any organization as well as in our interpersonal lives. Consequently, I decided to revise that first book, and focus more on those skills that I think are necessary for effectiveness within organizational environments as well as in life generally.

Over the last 45-plus years, I've trained virtually thousands of managers and individual contributors in the private and public sectors. Most of that work has been done in the government sector, predominantly with United States Department of Defense and Intelligence agencies. Over the years, I've received comments, both during and after training classes, that the skills the participants learned were skills that not only helped them when they went back to their jobs, but also in their personal lives. They found that these skills were helpful at home with their spouses, children, neighbors, relatives and other significantly important people. I remember, upon completion of a leadership communication class for the U.S. Navy, as I was packing up my computer, a participant approached me and said, "Ray, I don't know if you remember me, but I took a communication class from you thirteen years ago, and I want you to know that what I learned in that class really helped me in my career. The skills I learned undoubtedly helped me get promoted to Senior Executive Service (SES), and they also helped my marriage as well. I just wanted to thank you for what you did for me, and how much what you have to say means to me."

His comments truly humbled me. We shook hands; I thanked him for his kind words and expressed my appreciation that he would take the time to tell me that I had positively impacted his life. Isn't that what we all want, really? Don't we all want to have some positive impact on others? Having a positive impact on another person's life is one of the noblest and satisfying things that life can bring us. I have felt a great deal of gratification hearing and reading those kinds of comments from training participants, because they reinforced the realization that these skills have wide utility across organizational and interpersonal contexts. Even though the context may change, and the nature of the relationships may change, the fundamental principles and skills necessary to communicate effectively are still applicable no matter the circumstances.

I've started thinking more about my life, and how it has gone for my family and me. It became increasingly clear that these communication skills were beneficial in my own personal life, not just in terms of the organizational consulting and training that I've conducted over the last forty-five years, but also in terms of how our family has grown and become enriched by many of the skills that will be focused on in this book. I'm certainly the first to admit my many flaws and shortcomings, but I do believe that part of the reason I view my life as having some degree of success is because of the communication skills discussed in this book. Even though I have numerous flaws and have made more than my share of mistakes, I've been married for over fifty-eight years to the woman I consider the love of my life. We have borne three sons, who are truly good men, husbands, and fathers. What more can my wife and I ask for? In many ways, the way we measure the success of individuals is through the relationships that they have developed and nurtured, both professionally and personally.

I've come to believe that successful, long-term relationships are characterized by having **realistic expectations**; life has its ups and downs, and it's not always going to be easy. That realization helps people deal better with adversity. Having mutual, *realistic* expectations is important, but it needs to be coupled with the second characteristic which is **appreciation** for one another's uniqueness. Realistic expectaions coupled with appreciation for one another are significant characteristics of successful, long-term relationships. The third characteristic is being **absolutely supportive** of one another by acknowledging the other's views. It doesn't mean we must agree with everything. Even though disagreements occur, the parties continue to be supportive of one another by showing they care for them no matter what. Lastly, the fourth characteristic of successful, long-term relationships is characterized by both parties **not trying to change one another**. People are who they are—flaws and all. It's particularly important for both parties to accept one another, and not try to mold them into being someone else. I think we make a mistake when we try to "fix" people to be something other than themselves or when we try to make them the type of person, we want them to be. When we do this, the tendency is to focus on their faults or shortcomings rather than their strengths. For example, parents want their children to do well emotionally and academically in their preparation for adulthood. Certainly, it's important for parents to do what they can to help their children be successful, but if the parents' focus is on what their children are doing "wrong," they may not remember to focus on what their children are doing right, and not notice their unique strengths , and how they can be enhanced.

Supervisors and managers, I assume, also want their employees to succeed. After all, supervisors are essentially evaluated by how well their employees perform, so it's in their best interest to help their employees be successful. Consequently, effective supervisors and managers ensure their employees receive the proper technical and interpersonal training needed. However, even though some supervisors may be well intentioned, they may also make this mistake with their employees by trying to "fix" them by focusing on their weaknesses, rather than utilizing and leveraging the employees' strengths. Just as with children, employees don't necessarily need to be "fixed," they need support in order to develop.

However, let me be clear. This doesn't mean that parents should accept their children's development areas, and not try to help them improve, or that supervisors should accept an employee's shortcomings when the job requires new, more developed skills. In fact, I think it's a parent's and a supervisor's responsibility to help their children and employees be successful, but there needs to be an alignment between what the parent or supervisor wants and what the child or employee wants. It's when we try to "force fit" what we want without considering what the significant other person wants is when relationships usually run into trouble. Making an effort to get others to do things they really don't like or don't have an interest in, sets up a potentially adversarial relationship, rather than a supportive, nurturing one. It's usually best to find out what the other person is motivated to do or learn, and to show as much support as possible to develop those skills, rather than attempting to "fix" them so they become what we want them to be, instead of what they want to be. I think this holds true in organizational relationships and family relationships, including spousal relationships. Usually, when people are working for the same goals, and are aligned in their methods to develop those goals, things tend to work much better. One last point. I'm talking about skills for success in work and life. I'm not talking about supporting a child, employee, or spouse on something that may be detrimental to them interpersonally and in their job. We live in some very extraordinary times, and I don't wish to go down the cultural rabbit hole, but just because a child, employee, or spouse wants something that is obviously not going to be beneficial to them or to you, it is our responsibility to respectfully attempt to help them take a better path. Lastly, while I'm not equating employees as children, or children as employees, I'm attempting to show that the necessary skills required can be similar in both contexts.

Some of the examples used in this book will be based on the work that I have done with managers, supervisors, and individual contributors within public and private organizations, as well as examples employed in my own personal life. My intent is to show how those same skills can directly impact our relationships in a positive way. I've also decided not to make this an "academic" book. While the book's content is based on substantiated research, my own published and unpublished work, as well as my own experiences, I will not be citing numerous studies and references. I simply want to write something that might be helpful to the reader. So even though you won't see many citations and footnotes, I assure you that the content is supportable from a professional, academic, and personal perspective. It is my sincere hope that the principles and skills imparted in this book will help the readers both organizationally and personally.

Chapter 1

The Generic Nature of Communication:

It's Not Necessarily the Content. It's the Process.

As I said in the Preface, when I first wrote *The Guide to Better Communication in Government Service* in 1984, it was part of a Professional Communication series called ProCom, published by Scott Foresman. The idea of this series was that in various professions, the required communication skills needed to be different. In other words, a lawyer might require different communication skills than a physician, a financial consultant, a policeman, a nurse, or a government employee. Obviously, the content and technical information will be different, so it was assumed that the "communication process" must also be different. With this notion in mind, *The Guide to Better Communication in Government Service* was predominantly written for federal, state, and local government employees. Consequently, a fair amount of time was given to the distinction of government versus private sector organizations. While the features of public and private sector organizations may be different, they also share some commonalities. For example, the strategic goals of a public sector organization might be mission effectiveness, whereas in a private sector organization, it may be competitiveness as well as mission effectiveness. The financial goals of the public sector might be cost reduction and efficiency (good luck with that one); for private sector organizations, it would be profit, growth or market share. The values of public sector organizations might be accountability to the public, whereas private sector organizations may focus more on innovation, creativity, goodwill, and recognition. In public sector organizations, stakeholders may be taxpayers, and in private organizations, the stakeholders might be stockholders. Public sector organizations may be concerned with national security and political demands, and private sector organizations may be focused more on protection of intellectual capital and proprietary knowledge. The desired outcome of public sector organizations would be customer service. Private sector organizations would certainly have that as a primary outcome as well, or they may not remain in business. Customer service is a big issue in the public and private sectors. If customers are dissatisfied with a private, commercial organization, they can take their business elsewhere. However, in public sector organizations, customers don't usually have that option.

While many hardworking, dedicated public servants are out there, the reality is that the incentives are different regarding the need for effective customer service. While there are significant differences between public and private sector organizations, all of them require effective communication for them to succeed. Their managers must know how to build and nurture teams; they must know how to clearly articulate their decisions and their expectations; they must know how to give and receive effective feedback, and create an environment where employees feel appreciated and engaged; they must know how to conduct effective meetings, and present their ideas in the form of oral presentations and briefings; they must understand the importance of leadership and creating an environment of empowerment and accountability, and they must be able to think both critically and strategically to move their enterprises forward. We can see that while there are similarities and differences across public and private sector organizations, many similar communication responsibilities and skills are necessary for success.

So, while the particular profession, organizational type, and context define the *content* of the information conveyed, the communication of that information is a *process* that cuts across contexts, organizational types and professions. I think fundamental, generic skills are applicable no matter one's position or career. There may be more or less emphasis placed on certain skills, but regardless, whether you are in a public sector, private sector organization, or whether you are sitting around the dinner table talking with your spouse, your children, or friends and neighbors, there are fundamental, inherently important communication skills required no matter the context or the nature of those relationships. While much of my focus will be on organizational communication, I will also suggest how those same skills I write about can relate to our interpersonal lives as well. After all, don't we need to give feedback in a respectful way to our spouses? Don't we need to give feedback and articulate our expectations to our children and significant others in our lives? Don't we want to get along with our friends and neighbors? Don't forget our coworkers, bosses, and in-laws! Let's get started!

Chapter 2

The *"3 Things"* That Can Make All the Difference

Think about times when an interaction you've had with someone (at work or outside of work) went particularly well or poorly. As you think about the situation, try not to consider the topic or the content of the disagreement. Try to focus on the process. Depending on the example chosen, what were the things that made you feel good or bad about the situation? In my opinion, as you think about the circumstances, you will begin to focus on essentially three things. Were your *expectations* met or not? Did you feel you were being listened to, and your feelings and views were being *acknowledged*? Did you trust, or feel comfortable with the other person's *intentions?* All relationships center to one degree or another, on these three elements: **Expectations, Acknowledgment,** and **Intentions.** These three interdependent things affect all our interactions one way or another. Whether we are dealing with a customer service issue, discussing an issue with a work colleague, participating in team meetings, providing constructive feedback to a coworker or direct report, negotiating a purchase like a car or home, or discussing important issues with our spouses, our children, relatives, and other significant people in our lives. The **3 Things** affect every interaction in one way or the other, and to some degree or another. So, let's look at each one in more detail.

The First Thing: *Clear & Mutual Expectations*

Usually, when people have misunderstandings or a conflict with someone, it will center around a "violation of expectations." Take a moment and think about a recent situation where you and another person had a misunderstanding or conflict. It could be a job-related or personal issue. It could be a large or small issue. Regardless of the problem, I would bet that someone in the relationship violated an expectation. Either you did or said something that the other person didn't expect, or they did or said something that you didn't expect. Or—how about this one—the other person did something that you thought or felt was inappropriate. All relationships are a function of expectations. Usually, effective relationships are characterized by both parties being clear about what they can expect from one another. When expectations are mutually met, it tends to lead to more trust in the relationship. Think about times when people have said they would do something, and they didn't do what they said they would. Particularly when they agreed to do what you asked. When people violate an expectation, especially without explanation, or a flimsy excuse, trust is undermined in the relationship, leading to other problems. Whether you are a son, daughter, husband, wife, supervisor, or employee, if you say you are going to do something, and there is agreement, then you need to do it, and if you can't, explain why without making excuses or blaming others.

My wife and I have a second home in the Outer Banks of North Carolina. I remember years ago, my wife and I, and two of our three sons, went to the beach house for a week. Our middle son was serving in Iraq during Desert Storm at the time. Two of our sons asked if their girlfriends could join us. My wife and I said of course, and we had a good time at the beach together. There was an incident, however, that occurred a few days into the week that speaks to the importance of expectations. Our sons and their girlfriends said they would make the dinner for three days. However, they didn't clarify who was responsible for cleaning up afterward. On the first day, we had a nice meal together and the boys' girlfriends cleaned up the kitchen. The second day was the same. On the third day, the girlfriends were not happy campers. One of them blurted out "When are you guys going to help with the dishes? We're getting sick of doing all the work!" The boys looked a bit surprised and embarrassed, and one of them said "Why didn't you say something before? You cleaned up for two days, and you didn't seem upset about it. Why didn't you say something sooner? We don't mind helping!" (I'm not sure if I was in complete agreement with their "innocent" explanation, however.) What's important to note is that it's not a matter of who's right or wrong. What's important is that they didn't establish and discuss any expectations of one another before they decided to make dinner and clean up for three days. It might have been helpful to establish "ground rules" regarding who was responsible for what. Instead, the girls bit their lips and didn't say anything while they did both chores of making dinner and cleaning up afterward, each time getting increasingly upset about the boys' unwillingness to help. This example may appear to be a minor issue, but unclear expectations need to be addressed early or there will usually be misunderstandings in any relationship. This also means rather than withholding one's concerns, and not confronting the issue because we don't want to have an argument, or we don't want to upset the other person, we may only exacerbate the problem, and make it more difficult to resolve. In my opinion, it's usually best to confront a concern when it occurs rather than holding it in and becoming angrier by the minute. In a later chapter, I will address this issue when I talk about the "greater the need to communicate, the more difficult it becomes."

Reasonable Expectations in our Personal Relationships

I think it's important to distinguish expectations in our personal relationships versus our work relationships. On a personal level such as in a marriage or very close, loving relationship, your mutual expectations of one another should be treated with mutual respect, love, and support without trying to change the other person for who they are. Expecting the other person to react and feel the same way as we do, or to expect perfection from the other person, or for them to do things the same way as we do is a recipe for disaster in the relationship. Having expectations around the "rightness" or "wrongness" of doing certain things like household chores, keeping house, driving habits, eating habits, etc. will make conflict inevitable. Expectations without appreciation and support simply don't work very well. Showing respect through mutual expression of appreciation and acknowledgment is the glue that helps make a relationship long-lasting and strong.

Reasonable Expectations in the Work Environment

Let's consider the notion of clear and mutual expectations in the work environment. If you supervise, think back and ask yourself what you did the first few days after taking over a new team or project. What did you do to establish clear and mutual expectations with your new team or project for which you were now responsible? Did you sit down with them and discuss your expectations regarding how you wanted to work together? Did you talk about what was important and not important to you? Did you let them know your preferences regarding decision-making, communication, empowerment, feedback, and so on? Did you ask them what they expected of *you*? What they needed from you, and how you could help them be more successful? If you don't have these types of discussions early in the relationship, then people will fill in the blanks; they will often be wrong and there will likely be problems and misunderstandings. Taking the time to establish clear and mutual expectations early in relationships is always time well spent.

One more thing. In my opinion, having realistically high expectations of someone is being respectful to them, and having low expectations of someone is also a form of disrespect. I think that essentially, people tend to give you what you expect. If you don't expect much, that's what you get. Expectations should be mutual, *realistic* and *respectful* of the other person, thus leading to a more trusting, effective relationship.

The Second Thing: *Genuine Acknowledgment*

I believe one of the greatest needs that people have is the need for acknowledgment. Mark Twain once said, "**I can live for two months on a good compliment.**" This humorous quote from the wonderful Mark Twain may be more accurate than not. Compliments are incredibly important to people. They are a way of expressing our acknowledgment of others. For example, I love golf, and play as often as my schedule permits. Sometimes, I play nine holes, solo, just to practice and enjoy the outdoors. However, I much more enjoy playing 18 holes with friends who enjoy the game as much as I do. We express our joy and camaraderie by acknowledging one another's shots. "Good shot," "Great putt," etc. Of course, we also "razz" one another as well, but that's also a form of acknowledgment, because people don't playfully razz one another if they don't like them. "Banter" is very much a part of an expression of acknowledgment on the golf course, at work, or at home.

We can show acknowledgement at home, by remembering important dates; by saying "I love you" and "thank you" to our spouses, children, and significant others in our lives. We can tell others how much we appreciate what they **specifically** do. We can make coffee for our spouse in the mornings. We can write short notes thanking those who make life more enjoyable for us, for doing a good job, and for the little things that people do. We can put aside whatever we are doing to give our full attention to our spouse, our children, or our co-workers and employees. Years ago, I read somewhere that "gratitude is the path to joy." I think it's very important to be grateful for even the little things in life, and to express gratitude for what others do by acknowledging their efforts, their skills, their patience, their concerns, their support— and the list goes on. Finally, remember to "give more than take." Also remember that when you give, you do it selflessly, with no strings attached, and without expecting anything in return.

I want to emphasize the importance of being **genuine** when acknowledging someone. In my opinion, many managers make the mistake of giving positive feedback to someone no matter what it is that they've done. In other words, if the manager says "good job" no matter how well the person performed, the compliments become somewhat meaningless if everything the person has done is a "good job." With today's emphasis on feelings and positive reinforcement, managers may lose sight of the importance of constructive feedback. If employees are acknowledged for doing a "good job" even when they haven't done such a good job, two things could happen. They may begin to believe they are doing better than they actually are, and this distortion may lead to them becoming very upset during performance review discussions. The manager might hear "What do you mean I need to improve? You've been telling me all along that I've been doing a good job!"

Secondly, when people do substandard work, don't you think they often know it? If the manager tells employees that they've done a good job, and the employees know they really haven't, what does that do to the manager's credibility? The employees know they are essentially being lied to, which can undermine the manager's credibility and the relationship due to distrust. Additionally, if employees feel the manager's compliments are "canned" or forced, the compliment loses its meaning and becomes irrelevant. As a general rule, I have found that if you take any positive characteristic and carry it to the extremes on either end of the continuum, it will likely become a negative. Too much acknowledgement might appear disingenuous, and too little acknowledgement may lead to a lack of understanding of how one is doing in the job or the relationship, leading to unclear expectations and sense of worth.

Rule of thumb: If employees are doing a good job, absolutely acknowledge them for their work, and be specific in your feedback regarding what actions were performed well. However, if employees have not done a good job, acknowledge their effort, but also provide specific, constructive feedback. Discuss what needs to be done differently, what can be done to improve, what they've learned, and if they need your assistance. When someone doesn't do the job according to the manager's expectations, it is a perfect time to have a constructive coaching discussion.

Genuinely acknowledging others is the simplest way to develop and nurture our relationships at work, at home, and our daily lives. It truly can make a difference.

The Third Thing: *Clear Intentions*

The third thing that makes a difference in relationships is making our intentions clear when we are dealing with people. When our intentions are unclear or not trusted, our rapport with the other person can be undermined, and misunderstanding can occur. A few years ago, I was asked to be a facilitator for a work team that was having some internal problems. The team leader of the group asked if I would facilitate an offsite meeting at a location in Williamsburg, Virginia. I agreed to do it, and prior to the offsite, I conducted interviews with a few team members to get a better understanding of the issues. During one of the interviews, the interviewee said, "Excuse me, but I really need to talk about my team leader." I said "Sure. What about him?" Then she dropped the bomb. "I'll tell you what about him. I can't stand the guy!" I asked what he does or doesn't do that gave her those feelings, and she said "He doesn't even bother to say good morning. He walks right by and ignores me. I just can't stand the guy."

First of all, let me make it clear. In my opinion, she wasn't being very logical. Human, yes, but not necessarily logical. It is unfortunately "human" to draw conclusions about someone or something based on very limited data beyond our observations.

During the team building offsite, I usually try to deal with whatever issues crop up, and guess what—this issue came up. When the team member mentioned that the team leader ignores her, when walking by her workstation, he seemed surprised, and said "I'm sorry, but when I walk by, you often seem busy, and I don't want to bother you!" Who's "right" here? I guess it's based on where the behaviors are being "punctuated." From the team member's perspective, she was being ignored and probably disliked. From the team leader's perspective, he didn't want to bother her if she seemed busy.

There's another point to be made here. It's a safe assumption that when people observe our behavior, and they don't know our **intentions,** they often *assume* intentionality, and they may often assume the worst, based on what they see of our behavior. Let's see how it plays out. The intentions of the team leader are as follows: "She looks like she's busy, and I don't want to break her train of thought, so I won't interrupt her by saying good morning." From the team member's perspective, she's likely unaware of his intentions. The only thing she has to go on is his **behavior**, and it conveys a very different message to her. In her mind, she is likely processing the event in the following way: "He didn't say good morning again. Obviously, he's ignoring me (assuming his intent). If he's ignoring me, he's being inconsiderate, rude, and probably doesn't like me (Again, assumes his intent). Well, if he doesn't like me, then I don't like him. In fact, I can't stand the guy!"

It's imperative to understand this dynamic. As I said before, when people observe our behavior, and don't understand our **intentions**, they often assume intentionality and may assume the intent as negative. Consequently, they may act accordingly, by getting defensive, angry, withdrawn, etc. Remember this. **We judge OURSELVES by our INTENTIONS, but others judge us by our BEHAVIORS**. Generally speaking, people don't really know our intentions unless we tell them. If we don't make our intentions clear, the only thing they have to go on is our behavior. So, if we judge people solely on their behavior, without understanding their intentions, or if we don't make our intentions clear to people, a great deal of misunderstanding may occur. It can be as simple as stating your intentions before asking a question. For example, you might say "I know this is a concern of yours, and I want to understand" before asking a question. Or, you might say "I know how this issue is important to you, as it is to me. What needs to be done to resolve this issue?"

Our perception of another person's intentions has powerful impact on the viability and outcome of the relationship. For example, we've probably all dealt with a highly competent and knowledgeable salesperson who clearly explains the product, and what you can expect to pay for it. He or she acknowledges and answers your questions and is very considerate of your time and concerns. However, for some reason, you just don't trust the person, and you find yourself questioning his or **intentions**. That lack of trust in the person's intentions can be the deal breaker. The salesperson is very competent and does all the right things, but if you question his or her intentions, you question the person's integrity and good will toward you, and that's significant for any relationship.

Think of movie villains such as Hannibal Lector, Darth Vader, or Professor Moriarty. All of them are very intelligent, and good ole Hannibal and Moriarty could be downright charming. What was the one thing that you feared the most about the characters? It likely wasn't their intellect or their charm, it was their evil intent. This is what defines a villain. How we perceive a person's character is based on how we perceive their intentions. One's competence and interpersonal skills may be very appealing to us, but it's our perception of their intentions that attracts or repels us, and whether we trust them or not. Consequently, if you want to be influential with others, it's important that you reveal your intentions, and that they understand and trust your good intentions. You can better accomplish this by making an effort to do the following things:

- Overtly share your intentions by talking about what is important to you, your goals, and the values that drive your choices and decisions. Be willing to talk about how your experience forged your attitudes and values. We may make a big mistake to assume that people understand and trust our intentions. After all, we know we are honorable and well-intentioned, so they should know too, right? That kind of thinking can be a costly assumption. Our intentions are not always that obvious to others.

- State your intentions up front. You might say, "The reason I wanted to talk today is...". You can follow up by checking to see if your stated intent was understood by saying something like "Does that make sense?" If you had a prior discussion with someone, and you want to clarify or reconfirm the context of that discussion, you might say "I've been thinking about our discussion the other day, and if it's ok with you, I'd like to revisit that issue."

- Be consistent between what you say and what you do. Your stated intentions and how you behave daily with others must be consistent. It's extremely important to keep your word with others. I've said this before. If you say you will do something, then you must do it. That is being consistent. Also, if you ask for input or feedback from others, and then not listen to it, that is being inconsistent, and creates distrust. If you choose not to act on requested input from others, or take an action different from their recommendations, be sure to give the rationale for your decision. That's being consistent. Remember what I said earlier. We judge OURSELVES by our INTENTIONS, but others judge us by our BEHAVIORS.

I'm going to go as far as to say that all human interactions are influenced by these **"3 Things."** When you experience either positive or negative interactions and you are trying to analyze them, I believe you can get a much better understanding by focusing on how these **"3 Things"** occurred and interacted. Usually, when our relationships have gone well or poorly, we were either clear or unclear about our **expectations** of one another; we either did or didn't **acknowledge** the other person by validating and or respecting what they had to say; or we did or didn't make our **intentions** clear. If our intentions are misunderstood by the other person, it will influence the direction of the relationship. Closely considering **Expectations**, **Acknowledgment**, and **Intentions** is a helpful way to better understand why our relationships are going well--or not.

In my own consulting work, I am often asked to mediate a conflict between two or more coworkers. In those situations, I will focus on the "3 Things" to get the participants to explore their feelings and thoughts toward one another. How the "3 Things' manifest themselves differs based on the context, but I have found that I can always get at the root causes of the conflict by focusing on a (1) violation of expectations, (2) lack of acknowledgment, and (3) unclear or misinterpreted intentions.

Expectation Review

The "Expectation Review" is a tool that I've recommended to clients, and it's been helpful. Depending on the job, its complexity, and other extenuating circumstances, it's recommended that the manager and his or her direct report or team, formally meet on a regular basis. These meetings may be weekly, monthly, or quarterly, whichever seems most appropriate. The meetings will usually take twenty to thirty minutes, and they will follow a semi-structured agenda. The manager essentially asks the following four questions:

- **What's going well?**
- **What should we do more?**
- **What should we do less?**
- **What should we do differently?**

It's important that these questions become springboards for a dialogue. They should not be a request for a "report" from the employee or team. The questions allow for the manager and direct reports to discuss work-related issues in a positive, focused, and future-oriented manner. It's also important that the meeting be structured and held regularly according to the agreed-upon schedule so participants can prepare for them. Lastly, not every question needs to be explicitly asked, because they are sometimes addressed during the natural flow of dialogue.

These types of meetings can be beneficial by dealing with issues in a proactive manner. They are designed to clarify **Expectations**. They **Acknowledge** and empower the employees' worth by requesting their input, and they make it clear that the manager's **Intentions** are focused on improvement, not blame. If you notice, nowhere in the four questions is the word "problem" used. Informal variations of the "Expectation Review" can be used at home as well, when various home and school projects are being discussed, or when a family member takes on a new job, and so forth.

Before going to the next chapter, take a moment to consider a work or personal relationship which is important to you, and analyze that relationship according to how you think you manage **mutual expectations, genuine acknowledgment**, and **clear intentions**. This analysis could give you valuable insight into the viability of that relationship. Ask yourself these questions: "What do I do to make my expectations clear with this person?" "What do I do to understand their expectations of me?" "What do I do to acknowledge what this person does or doesn't do?" "Is my acknowledgment genuine?" "What do I do to make my intentions clear to this person?" "Have there been times when this person seemed to question my intentions?" If the reason you chose the person to consider was because you are having some difficulties with that individual? My guess is that it's because one or more of the 3 Things are involved.

Chapter 3

Five Basic "Laws" of Communication

Regardless of the context and the nature of the relationship that you're in, there are communication principles that will impact your effectiveness. In this chapter, we will look at certain communication "laws" that can affect our organizational and personal relationships.

Law #1: You Cannot Not Communicate!

We are "walking messages". It's not a question of communicating or not communicating, it's a matter of at what level we're communicating. Sometimes, it's not **what** you say, but **how** you say it that impacts others. On the other hand, it may be what you don't say, or your silence that can speak volumes. One thing is certain. The higher up one goes in the organization, the more everything one does (or doesn't do) is scrutinized and evaluated by others. In organizations, if we get promoted to a supervisory, managerial, or team leader role, those who were our coworkers yesterday may now be our direct reports today. They will begin to look at you quite differently when you take on a new role. Based on your new role and the expectations that come with it, their expectations and others' views of you will change. Consequently, your communication behavior toward other members of the organization may well have to be modified to be more consistent with your new role. What you say or what you don't say, how visible you are, how you make decisions, how you resolve differences, how you conduct yourself in meetings, how you make presentations, how you brief people, give them important feedback, and keep them informed are all being evaluated whether you're doing these things or not. Again, we are communicating whether we want to or not. Additionally, our communication occurs at different levels:

The first is the intra-personal level; the communication takes place internally. It consists of the relationship we have with our environment. It takes form in the attitudes, values, beliefs, and internal reactions we have toward all kinds of stimuli existing in our surroundings.

The second level is the interpersonal level. This consists of our one-to-one communication in our daily interpersonal situations with our managers, coworkers, direct reports, spouses, friends, children and significant others. It consists of our behavior, both verbal and nonverbal.

The third level is the small group level. This consists of communication, which occurs in small groups of people whether work-related or non-work related. While our communication is interpersonal in nature, because small groups often possess some formal structure and purpose, it may be more appropriate to classify it as a distinct level.

The fourth level is the organizational level, which consists of the interdependent relationships of interpersonal and group interactions as we move toward larger system goals. The organizational level consists of the formal and informal processes that take place within an organizational system that help the system achieve its goals.

No matter what level of communication is taking place, no matter what we are doing or not doing, we are sending messages to others. For example, a lack of feedback to a direct report, is still feedback. It may be telling your direct report that you don't care enough to provide the feedback they may need. Also, in our interpersonal lives, when we are being observed interacting with our spouses, children, relatives, etc., we are also being evaluated on how those interactions go. We are not only "walking messages," we are also "walking role models" to our employees, team members, spouses, children, friends, and other significant people in our lives. Consequently, on some level, we are being observed and are being evaluated by what we are doing or not doing—whether we like it or not.

Law #2: Information is Power (Potentially)

Max Weber, often referred to as the "Father of Bureaucracy," wrote that organizational power was vested in the legality of the office. According to Weber, it was the power of the position that allowed one to have influence in the organizational bureaucracy. However, any member of a modern organization realizes authority is not the only factor that gives someone power and influence. In addition to the formal network, there is an informal network that operates in all organizations, with informal leaders who may never appear on the traditional organizational chart. However, they often possess a good deal of organizational information. They are the "gatekeepers" who, because of their role, may possess a great deal of information regarding the workings of the organization. Often, administrative and executive assistants are in positions that allow them to process and filter a great deal of information regarding decisions, organizational direction and strategy.

For example, a number of years ago, I was part of a team of researchers who conducted an organizational communication audit of a large school system in Florida. Some of our findings showed that many of the "gatekeepers" of information were people that worked in the school administration warehouse! It seemed that a great deal of organizational information went through them. They knew more about organizational decisions and the formal and informal goings-on than many of the principals!

It's important to remember that one's "legal authority" can certainly have an impact when attempting to influence others, but it can only go so far in being truly influential. One's influence is also a function of the information possessed, and how that information is articulated to others in order to influence their behavior. That's why it's so important for managers to keep their employees up-to-date and appropriately informed on policies and decisions.

Law #3: Words Have No Meaning—People Do.

"Meaning" can be understood two ways: "connotative" meaning or associative meaning, and "denotative" or operational meaning. Denotative meanings are basically dictionary definitions, the agreed-upon meanings attributed to words in our culture. Although a word may have a fairly stable meaning, that does not eliminate problems for people who use the word, because nearly all words have multiple usages. The average educated adult uses about 2,000 words in daily interaction, and the 500 most commonly used words have over 14,000 dictionary definitions! Even though we have our iPhones available, we usually deal with others on the level of connotative meaning. These are the thoughts, feelings, and perceptions that we have about a word. And, since we are all different, we will bring differing degrees of meaning to a word no matter what the word may be.

Many of our most familiar words are abundant with connotative meaning. Words such as mother, father, politics, religion, happiness, love, success, are full of personal interpretations regarding their meaning. It is important to realize that as words become more abstract, the more difficult it is to achieve mutually agreed-upon meaning. Consequently, the word is not the "thing." It only *represents* the thing. Virtually all words have denotative and connotative meaning. The type and degree of reaction that humans give to the words will vary from one person to another. Meanings reside not in the words, but in the minds of those who use them or are exposed to them.

In both public and private sector organizations, words are notoriously used in ambiguous ways to describe mission, vision, programs, projects and initiatives. The use of bureaucratic terms has been referred to as "bureaucratese," which is all too common for many of us. Bureaucratese often sounds good or very important, but it doesn't always advance understanding of what they are truly about. Take a look at the following three columns. Match any three words from the three columns. See what you come up with. The three words you choose may not make much sense, but I bet they will sound official and be at their "bureaucratese" best.

Column 1	Column 2	Column 3
1. Integrated	1. Management	1. Options
2. Total	2. Organizational	2. Flexibility
3. System-atized	3. Monitored	3. Capability
4. Parallel	4. Reciprocal	4. Mobility
5. Functional	5. Digital	5. Program-ming
6. Responsive	6. Logic	6. Concept
7. Optical	7. Transitional	7. Projection
8. Synchro-nized	8. Incremental	8. Hardware
9. Compatible	9. Third Genera-tion	9. Contingen-cy
10. Balanced	10. Policy	10. Initiative

In organizations, we use "bureaucratese" and acronyms to communicate with one another, and I'm pretty confident that much relevant information is lost in the translation. We may need to remind ourselves to think of language not as reality, but as a code to help us describe reality, made up differently by different people in different places. For example, terms such as "woke" "equity" "inclusion" "social justice" have very different meanings for people along the political spectrum. For me at least, one may decide to call a chair a table, but to me, it's still a chair. As I said earlier. I also choose not to go down that rabbit hole.

We also use certain phrases that have become cliché. Personally, I am so tired of hearing "At the end of the day," "I've got a lot on my plate," "Reaching out," "Going forward" or "Circling back," that I find myself leaning toward cynicism and not listening when those phrases are being uttered. Sometimes, speaking plainly and directly can be challenging in many of today's organizations.

Law #4: The Greater the Need to Communicate, the More Difficult it Becomes

This law of communication may well be another human dilemma. Let's look at what it says a bit more closely. Whenever we have problems in our relationships, usually it's because we are not communicating very effectively with each other, and we may realize that it's becoming increasingly necessary to confront the issues and deal with them. We may also know that we should say to the other person, "Let's sit down and talk about the problem." Ironically, as the need to discuss the problem increases, so does the difficulty to do it! I think we sometimes forget that the need and the difficulty to communicate are often synonymous because our emotions, biases and perceptions get in the way of our ability to deal with issues rationally. If we didn't have a great need to communicate, it probably wouldn't be as difficult. As the need increases, often, so does the difficulty.

For example, how many of us have had a direct report, manager, spouse, or significant other relationship with whom we have real communication problems? Over time, unless the problems are confronted, we will tend to develop increased concern, and notice things that bother us more and more about the person. I remember having a consulting job where I worked with two employees who were having real problems in their working relationship. When I asked one of them what bothered her about the other person, she said she "couldn't stand the way he slurps his coffee," among other things. When the need to communicate becomes greater, the little things tend to become the big things, distort our focus, and make it more difficult to address issues or concerns.

These perceptions will invariably become distorted and affect our ability to discuss the problem rationally. Consequently, there is the tendency to avoid one another if possible, have periodic flare-ups, or allow our anger to spill over into our other relationships. Now we will likely be at a point where the greater the need to sit down and have a rational discussion about our concerns, the more difficult it has become! Healthier relationships are often characterized by the parties addressing issues as they occur, rather than letting them fester. They are also characterized as being non-judgmental, open, and direct with one another about their concerns. That is often easier said than done. Later on, I'll suggest some ways to do just that.

Law #5: The Nature of a Relationship Is Contingent upon the Punctuation of the Communicational Sequence between the Communicants.

How's that for a non-communicative message about communication! Let me for a moment, explain another "human dilemma." Just as we punctuate syllables in words to give them emphasis, we also tend to punctuate events in order to give them emphasis. However, *where* we punctuate these events determines our "reality" about the events. I know that explanation doesn't help much, so let me give a couple examples: The husband nags because the wife withdraws, doesn't speak up, doesn't talk, doesn't whatever (husband's punctuation). On the other hand, the wife withdraws and doesn't speak up because the husband nags (wife's punctuation). Let's also look at this in an organizational context: The team leader doesn't like a particular team member because the member never speaks up in meetings and doesn't seem to be a "team player" (team leader's punctuation). The team member doesn't participate in meetings and doesn't feel a part of the team because the team leader doesn't like him (team member's punctuation).

In summary, as managers, individual contributors, spouses, parents, friends, we are indeed "walking messages" communicating on some level whether we want to or not. If you manage, you _are_ the organization to your direct reports, and how you communicate with your people will determine to a large degree, how they view and feel about the organization. It often boils down to how we develop and nurture our relationships. Close attention to how you are communicating both verbally and nonverbally can have a dramatic effect on performance and effectiveness. Choose your words wisely and give consideration to the basic "Laws" of communication outlined in this chapter, and don't be reticent to request feedback from others on how things are going at work, with your manager, team members, direct reports and customers. You might also try to solicit more feedback from your spouse, children, and other significant people in your life. You may get confirming responses, and you may also get responses that will surprise you and move to a better understanding. We might take a moment to reflect and assess where and when we tend to punctuate events inappropriately, and how these events have made us less effective communicators in both our organizational and personal lives. Having a better understanding of the five "Laws" can help us understand why our relationships are working well or not. They are worth paying attention to.

Chapter 4

Why Can't We Talk to Each Other Anymore?!?: The Need for Critical Thinking Skills

I want to warn the reader up front that I'm going to take a very personal approach to some of the content in this chapter and may offend some readers. However, I also hope my words will stimulate honest discussion of where our society is heading. With that said, it seems there was a time when people would be able to sit and talk about politics, philosophy, sports, religion, and various life issues. Sometimes the discussions would become heated, but afterwards, people were able to still laugh at and with one another and remain friends. From my perspective, this interpersonal dynamic is vanishing before our eyes. It's becoming increasingly difficult for people to engage in heated but rational discussions without becoming overly upset, resulting in a damaged relationship. This increasing inability to discuss various issues has negatively affected long-standing relationships, families, work teams, etc. Some of this may be due to the increasingly hostile political environment, social and cultural changes, and revisionist history taking place in the country. As an anecdotal example, our golf group (We call ourselves the "Gaggle") has decided not to discuss politics in our email correspondence or when we get together for a drink after a round of golf. It seems more difficult for people to form cogent arguments, and respectfully ask questions for clarification. Instead, it seems there's more of a tendency to speak in absolutes without supporting evidence for one's position. We seem to be more socially isolated from one another. Some of this may be due to the isolation many experienced because of COVID lockdowns, masking, and the closing of schools, churches, and businesses. This social isolation has had a profound impact on our society. Unfortunately, we may have lost the intellectual and interpersonal competencies of a generation of young people.

Additionally, cultural upheaval and change have disrupted long-standing traditions and norms, often leading to more isolation and division. The assault on language and free speech has made people unsure and worried about what is "politically correct" from one day to the next. Acceptance or rejection of certain words, often make people unsure of what is "appropriate", and ambiguity around language tends to make people more reticent and apprehensive to discuss issues openly. Being hesitant or unable to speak freely is a very slippery slope. Being able to think critically, and speak our minds is at the forefront of a free society and should be cherished and protected.

Social isolation and diminishing interpersonal skills may also be due to the overuse and dependence on technology at the expense of interpersonal relationships. I remember a few years ago, I was in Pensacola, Florida working for the Navy. One evening I decided to have dinner at a local seafood restaurant. While I was waiting for my meal to be served, a family of three adults and three teenagers sat at a large table across from me. As soon as they sat down, they ALL took their phones out. I decided to linger a bit so I could unobtrusively observe them. The only time I saw them speak was when they were ordering their meals. Even while they were eating, they didn't speak to one another! When they finished their meals, they went back to their phones until the waiter came with a check. What a shame this was to me. Here was a beautiful family, likely on vacation, hopefully having a good time visiting Florida, losing the opportunity to interact with one another because of the preoccupation with their phones and social media. The scene represented a problem of our times for me.

Lastly, and not insignificantly, our educational system is partially at fault for an increasing inability to think critically and for the undermining of interpersonal competencies. For approximately the last 60 years our educational system and universities have taught what might be referred to as "situational ethics." This approach focuses on the situation dictating to a large degree the "rightness" or "wrongness" of our actions. The focus is on the circumstances of the situation rather than logical, ethical, or traditional standards of morality and justice. During this time "non-directive" psychotherapy also became very popular. It was based on the notion of being totally non-judgmental of another person's behavior. After all, "who am I to judge another person?" As a college professor for over thirty years, I got caught up in this philosophy as well. The focus shifted from fundamental first principles and factual knowledge to the focus on feelings and emotions. (2 + 2 doesn't equal 5, but do you feel good about it?). This thinking has led us to the philosophy that everyone gets a trophy. There are no winners or losers. Everyone is a winner. The focus is on the self. This sounds nice, but it's not very realistic. Life will always have winners and losers. Not everyone can be a winner. Life is not always easy. In my opinion, this type of thinking has led to a good deal of narcissism and self-centeredness. This shift toward feelings over logic has led many to be easily offended if someone disagrees with them and their views. Questioning someone has become viewed as a personal attack, making someone feel "unsafe" or "offended." This shift toward feelings over substance makes it very difficult to approach issues in a thoughtful, critical manner that focuses on logic and facts. To a large degree, the focus is on the notion that someone else is responsible for how a person feels. I want to be clear here. I am responsible for how I feel, think, and behave. No one else is responsible for those three things except me. They are the choices that I make. I may not like what someone else says or does, but I'm responsible for how I *respond* to them— no one else. Placing our feelings on to others is relinquishing our individuality and freedom, making it very difficult to think critically, and have meaningful conversations about sensitive issues.

Now that I've gotten that off my chest, let's take a closer look at what critical thinking is, what are some of its challenges, and how we can improve our critical thinking skills.

What is Critical Thinking?

The term "critical" comes from the Greek word *kritikos* meaning "able to judge or discern."

Therefore, critical thinking may be defined as the type of interpretive thinking that questions, analyses, evaluates before making a judgement about what is said, heard, or written.

Think about times when you or your team grappled with a problem at work, or when you and your family had a difficult decision to make. A fair amount of evidence suggests that the more systematic and collaborative we are in these situations, the more effective we will be in our problem-solving decision-making. So, whether we are at work or at home, being more systematic and collaborative in our approach to problems enhances our ability to see all sides of an issue, and allows us to hear alternative views and insights, often leading to better decisions. Critical thinking in these types of situations consist of systematically considering different aspects of a problem, considering various points of view, asking questions, and gathering and analyzing information before making decisions. This process consists of two types of thinking: *Divergent* thinking and *Convergent* thinking. Divergent consists of brainstorming ideas where all ideas, no matter how far-fetched, is acknowledged and recorded. The process is to get all ideas out in front of people. Convergent thinking is taking all those ideas and systematically exploring them until they converge into a thoughtfully considered solution or decision. For this process to be successful, participants must rely on their critical thinking and communication skills. However, because we are human, critical thinking can be elusive for several reasons. There are many things that affect our ability to analyze problems and make decisions. Let's take a look at just a few.

- ***There's an emotional dimension to every thought we have and every decision we make.*** Like it or not, we are not Mr. Spock. Our emotions and egos can easily affect our thinking about issues, and they often do. We always need to be on guard to not allow them to negatively affect our logical thinking, and it's much easier said than done.

- ***People Tend to Seek Out and Validate Evidence That Supports Their Beliefs and Decisions, While <u>Discounting</u> Evidence That Does Not.*** It is very natural for people to seek out evidence and information that supports their decisions or views. This is why people tend to read certain books, magazines, and newspapers, or view certain websites or television networks, and discount sources that tend to oppose those views. There's a tendency to seek out sources of information that provide support for how we view things regarding our values, attitudes and beliefs, and a tendency to discount those sources that don't. This only reinforces our existing views and biases, and it's unfortunately very human to do so. Years ago, my wife and I used to subscribe to both the Washington Post and the Washington Times. Sometimes, we would spread the two papers out on the kitchen table and compare their headlines. We would look at what was above the fold and below the fold, what stories were in the front sections and the back sections of the papers, and what each paper considered to be important and unimportant news. At times, we were truly amazed. It was as if we were reading about two different worlds! I found it to be a useful exercise because it forced us to examine alternative perspectives on issues that were important to us. I will admit however, that we only receive one of those newspapers today, but I won't say which one. The tendency to seek out information that supports one's views is referred to as **"confirmation bias."** This manifests itself when we only read certain material, only watch certain television networks, only listen to certain politicians and pundits, etc., and avoiding or discounting all other sources of information that don't coincide with our views. This can lead to a very narrow and distorted view of reality.

- ***People tend to cling to their beliefs in the face of contradictory evidence.****There may be many reasons why people tend to cling to their beliefs in the face of contradictory evidence. One of the factors is an initial commitment to the idea (true believers) and another is receiving social support from significant others to continue believing something. This clinging to one's beliefs is called **"belief perseverance."** The irony of this, is that one's beliefs may even be strengthened when others attempt to present evidence refuting them. This phenomenon is known as the **"backfire effect."**

- ***People tend to view the around them in terms of patterns.*** This is a very old exercise, and some of you may have seen it before. With that said, try doing the following exercise below anyway. Please connect all 9 dots on the page with 4 straight lines, without raising your pen or pencil from the page.

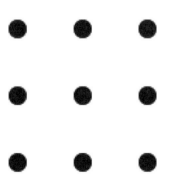

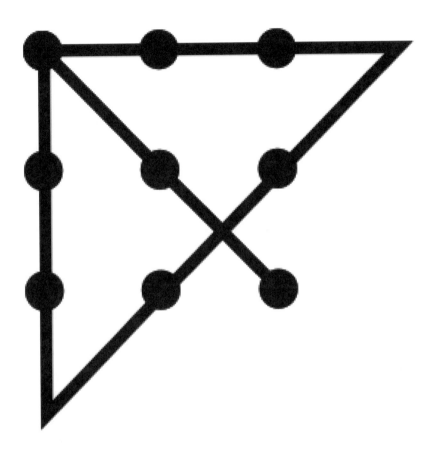

The above drawing is one option for connecting all the dots with 4 straight lines without raising their pen or pencil from the page. Even though this is an old exercise, and some people may have seen it before, they still may have difficulty with it. Remember, I said that people tend to see things around them in terms of patterns? When people look at the nine dots, they tend to "see" a square or box and try to force the four lines into that pattern. There is a tendency for people to constrain themselves by the pattern their minds have created. Remember, when you were in kindergarten, and the teacher would tell you to make sure you "stayed within the lines" when you were coloring various pictures in your coloring book? That type of thinking tends to carry over to our adult lives when we are thinking in terms of patterns. We tend to force fit what we see, hear, think, and feel into patterns that make sense to us. It's interesting to note that the term "thinking outside of the box" originated from this exercise. Of course, this phrase has come to mean we must be creative in the way we are approaching a problem or issue, and not get stuck in traditional thinking about the issue.

The reality is that, as human beings, our thinking is very fragile. There is always an emotional dimension that can both negatively and positively affect our thinking and judgment; our unconscious biases influence our conscious thinking; we tend to seek out and validate evidence that supports our beliefs and decisions, and discount evidence that doesn't support those beliefs, even when we are faced with evidence to the contrary; and we can get stuck in patterns of thought that may limit our creativity, problem-solving and decision-making abilities. So, what can we do about these frailties that we all have to some degree, and how can we become better critical thinkers? First, remember that a successful critical thinker doesn't critically evaluate the person. The focus is on critically evaluating the ideas and information. This distinction is extremely important. Critically evaluating people leads to defensiveness and conflict, whereas critically evaluating information and ideas can lead to better understanding and clarity. The purpose of critical thinking is not to be "right," but rather to gather and assess the right information. Much of this can be achieved by practicing the following three characteristics: *Curiosity, Flexibility*, and *Re-Framing.* Let's take a look at each one in a bit more detail.

Characteristic #1: Curiosity

One of the best ways to practice this characteristic is to think like a child. Remember when you were young, and everything seemed new and exciting, and life seemed to hold endless possibilities? Remember when your favorite question (often to the dismay of many adults) was "why" or "how"? Here are some strategies to increase your curiosity:

- **Banish "know-it-all" attitudes and negativity.** My Italian grandfather used to say, "Know-it-alls who don't know what they're talking about are a pain in the--neck (He used a more colorful word), and Know-it-alls who do know what they're talking about are merely less of a pain in the neck."

- **Make an effort to remove some of your pre-conceived notions.** This can be very challenging, but it's important to not allow pre-conceptions to influence our thinking. When we allow our pre-conceptions to influence our thinking, we tend to develop self-fulfilling prophecies, and may often be wrong.

- **Ask questions and consider new ideas and conclusions.** The ability to ask good questions is at the heart of effective critical thinking. Too often a non-critical thinker will accept information as fact, rather than asking for more clarity. I have found one of the best questions to ask when a statement is made as a fact without supporting evidence is "How do we know?" Other types of questions to ask are "Why" questions, or "What" or "How" questions. In order to minimize the possibility of people getting defensive by your questions, get in the habit of acknowledging the other person before asking the question. For example, you might say, "That's an interesting idea. Why do you feel it's so important?" or "That's a good point. What led you to that conclusion?" or "That's a good idea. How do you think it will be implemented?" Getting into the habit of acknowledging the other person before asking a question for clarification minimizes the tendency for the other person to get defensive and leads to more effective dialogue. The subtleties of effectively asking questions can also be significant. For example, the difference between "why" questions and "what" questions can be very subtle. Let's say I sell real estate (I don't), and I had potential buyers look at a house, and I want to know if they liked it or not. I might ask them if they saw the house, and how they liked it. Their response might be "We didn't like it very much." My next logical question might be "Why not?" This seems fine, but the "why" question sounds as if I'm asking the potential buyers to justify their feelings about the house, and I'm sure they will come up with something to justify their statement. Notice the difference if I ask, "What is it about the house that you didn't like?" Now I'm asking for information instead of justification. This may sound minor, but people feel more comfortable providing requested information rather than justifying their opinions.

- **Don't allow pride or ego get in the way of clear thinking.** When our ideas are being questioned, we must be very careful not to allow our pride or ego to keep us from listening what the other person is saying. When our ideas and opinions are being critically evaluated, we might interpret the questions as a personal attack on our intellect or character. This can lead us to a situation where we may be unwilling to listen and refuse to reflect on an issue because our egos and self-esteem are being threatened. One of the things I've been asked to do in my consulting business was to attend various executive meetings and observe the interaction and group process. I would then make my observations known to the group for them to reflect on. During some of these meetings, I would often observe the number of times egos would get in the way of effective problem solving. I would see very smart people dig in their heels, unwilling to consider alternative views because their egos and self-esteem were being threatened, not necessarily because they thought they were right. Consequently, ineffective decisions were sometimes made, not based on logical argument, but because of bruised egos and pride.

Characteristic #2: Flexibility

There are numerous ways to exhibit flexibility in our relationships at work and home. One way is to make a conscious effort to consider alternative points of view. One can do this by considering various sides of an issue, by expanding one's sources of news events, and by reading information from different sources. This may not be as easy as it seems because it can be disruptive of our frame of reference, and how we might see the world. Another way to exhibit our flexibility is by making a greater effort to solve problems through consensus and collaboration. This often requires the ability to deal with ambiguity without getting overly stressed, and the ability to be adaptive to unexpected and changing conditions. The opposite of being flexible and working collaboratively with others is the need for certainty, resistance to ambiguity, and a reluctance to consider alternative views other than our own. Working through problems in a collaborative manner and trying to reach consensus can be stressful and time-consuming, but it's usually worth it.

Characteristic #3: Reframing

Reframing is less of a characteristic, and more of a technique or strategy actually. It's sometimes referred to as Cognitive Reframing. It's a technique used to shift our mindset so we're able to look at a situation, person, group, or relationship from a somewhat different perspective. For example, we might look at an organizational change initiative or a change in our personal lives as a crisis. If those changes are reframed, we might view them as potential opportunities. Reframing can be a powerful way to view things from a different vantage point, which may lead to very different conclusions. The fundamental idea is the frame through which we view a situation determines our point of view or perspective. When that frame is shifted, the meaning, thinking, and behavior often change with it.

When we consider the **"3 Things"** in a relationship, we have likely drawn conclusions about what we expect from the other person, we have likely concluded whether the other person has sufficiently **acknowledged** us, and we have likely concluded what we think the other person's **intentions** are towards us. If we are expecting difficulties in the relationship, we may try reframing our perceptions of those three things to reassess the accuracy of how we are viewing the relationship. Sometimes reframing the 3 things can be a powerful tool in getting us to re-evaluate our supposition about others and our relationships with them. Remember also, to be curious and flexible in the way we think about things by banishing our "know it all" attitudes, asking questions, not allowing our pride and egos get in the way of our thinking by considering various point of view, and working collaboratively with others while striving for consensus in our decisions. Here is a chart showing how you might consider reframing as a way of viewing problems and issues.

Reframing: Two Ways of Looking at a Problem

Presenting Problem	Reframed Problem
It's them	It may be us.
It's a problem	It's an opportunity.
Our goal is unachievable	We don't have our goal broken into realistic steps.
Our idea/product won't sell	We may not be sending the right message.
We don't have enough resources	We may be wasting the resources we do have.
We need to gather more input	We may need to pay more attention to the input we're already getting.
Our employees don't care	Our employees may not have enough time/resources to do a quality job.
We don't have enough money	We haven't identified new sources of money, or wasting what we have.
We can't get along with each other	We haven't committed to working through our concerns with one another.
We don't have enough time to do all these things	We have to decide what to do now and what to do later.

As you look at both columns, place a check mark next to the ones that you find yourself saying or thinking, and try re-framing them. The process of doing so could change the way you are defining an issue of importance to you.

Universal Questions that help our Thinking

(Remember, it's usually a good idea to ACKNOWLEDGE the other person before asking many of these questions.)

Clarity
Could you elaborate further?
Could you give me an example?
Could you illustrate what you mean?

Accuracy
How could we check on that?
How could we find out if that is accurate?
How could we verify or test that?

Precision
Could you be more specific?
Could you give me more details?

Relevance
How does that relate to the problem?
How does that bear on the question?
How does that help us with the issue?

Depth
What factors make this a difficult problem?
What are some of the complexities of this issue?
What are some of the difficulties we need to deal with?

Reframing
Do we need to look at this from another perspective?

Do we need to consider another point of view?
Do we need to look at this in other ways?

Logic
Does all this make sense together?
Does the solution actually solve the problem?
Does what we conclude follow from the evidence?

Significance	Is this the most important problem to consider?
	Is this the central idea to focus on?
	Which of these facts are most important?
(Questions to ask ourselves) Self-Assessment	Do I have a vested interest in this issue?
	Am I sufficiently considering the viewpoints of others?
	Am I letting my pride or ego get in the way of my thinking?

As I said earlier in this chapter, in my opinion, our educational system has failed us by getting away from fundamentals and focusing too much on feelings and politically correct speech. Unfortunately, many of our children matriculate through high school without a solid foundation in English, reading and writing proficiency, mathematics, civics, and history. Additionally, because of the focus on feelings over logic, many students do not possess an understanding of logic, argumentation, and an awareness of logical fallacies. Because of these limitations, many of our students enter the adult world lacking an understanding of how to formulate an argument and are susceptible to fallacious thinking as they are exposed to mass media, social media, and political discourse. Additionally, this susceptibility to fallacious thinking makes it more difficult to have productive discussions around politics, culture, historical and contemporary world events, work issues, interpersonal issues with family members and with significant others in our lives. Consequently, it would be helpful to look more closely at fallacious thinking and logical fallacies that we are all exposed and susceptible to daily.

Logical Fallacies

I'm sure we've all heard an argument or statement that was presented as if it were a fact, but it didn't seem to be accurate or true. Maybe the statement of a problem rang true, but the solution to the problem didn't seem to logically follow, or it wasn't validated to your satisfaction. This example represents what is sometimes called a *Non Sequitur* fallacy. This is when the conclusion is not necessitated by the premise. Essentially all fallacies fall under the umbrella of a *Non Sequitur*. Let's take an example. Suppose I said that "Everyone in our country should have access to a quality education." It's safe to assume that we would all agree with that statement or premise. Then, what if I followed up with "Therefore, we should all support this large federal educational program." In this example, the conclusion drawn is not necessitated by the premise. While we may agree with the premise that everyone should have access to a quality education, a federal education program may only be one of many options for that to be accomplished. For example, privatizing education, or allowing the states to have more control over the unique educational requirements in their respective states may be a better solution than federalizing education in which "one size fits all." Regardless, the point is that drawing a potentially fallacious conclusion based on a valid premise is at the essence of a *Non- Sequitur.* Another example of a *Non Sequitur* fallacy is to say something like this. "Everyone in our country should feel safe from bodily harm. Therefore, we should amend the Constitution, and disallow gun ownership because guns cause bodily harm." While I certainly agree that we should all feel safe from bodily harm, amending the Constitution, and not allowing citizens to exercise their Constitutional rights is not the only conclusion to support that premise--far from it. Greater emphasis on law enforcement, higher standards for purchasing a gun, more gun safety education might be considered as well. As can be seen from these two examples, *Non Sequiturs* make claims that don't necessarily support an agreed upon premise. They also tend to focus on solutions instead of looking at the causes of a problem. If we focus on the solution prior to defining the problem, the solution could **become** the problem. Additionally, *Non Sequiturs* might also focus on an unsupportable cause of a problem. For example, when a hurricane or a wildfire hits an area, a news story might say they were caused by "global warming." First, while global warming may be of legitimate concern, the reality is that hurricanes have always existed, and in many cases, with more devastating results, and the jury is still out regarding evidence that global warming "causes" hurricanes. Wildfires have always existed as well, and rather than global warming being the "cause," one might consider and be open to discuss the possibility that the lack of controlled burning, and the accumulation of underbrush due to environmental regulations and restrictions can make forests virtual tinderboxes. Additionally, the accumulation of underbrush makes it difficult for firefighters to access the stricken area, thus causing the fire to get out of control. There are many more examples one could give that represent *Non Sequiturs*. We are being bombarded with them every day in the media, social media, "fake news," and unfortunately, even in our classrooms. When someone draws a conclusion regarding a cause or solution to a problem, we might respectfully ask for supporting evidence to their claim.

Rule of thumb: When opinions are stated as facts, and those opinions are not confirmed, we run the risk of diminishing the likelihood of productive dialogue.

Other Common Fallacies

When having a discussion with someone in an attempt to get at an answer or an explanation, we may encounter a person who commits logical fallacies. Such discussions may prove frustrating and futile. You might try asking for evidence and independent confirmation or provide other hypotheses that give a better or simpler explanation. The following briefly describes some of the more common fallacies.

- **Ad hominem**: Latin for "to the man." An arguer who uses *ad hominem,* attacks the person instead of the argument. Whenever an arguer cannot defend his or her position with evidence, facts, or reason, he or she may resort to attacking a person or group either through labeling, name-calling, offensive remarks and anger. Unfortunately, we see this far too often in the political arena. *e.g., "Don't pay any attention to him. He doesn't know what he's talking about."*

- **Argument based on fear**: An argument based on an appeal to fear or a threat. We saw some of this during the COVID pandemic *e.g., "If you don't support this, disastrous effects will occur."* (Never let a crisis go to waste)

- **Argument based on emotion**: An argument aimed to sway popular support by appealing to sentimental weakness rather than facts and reasons *e.g. "You must support this program. After all, it's for the children."*

- **Hasty Generalization**: Drawing a general conclusion based on limited information. *e.g., "Smoking isn't hazardous. My parents smoked all their lives and they never got sick from it."* Or: *"I don't like France. I once had a really bad experience in a restaurant in Paris."* Simply because someone can point to an event or a few favorable or unfavorable experiences doesn't necessarily mean that an overall conclusion can be legitimately made. **Be careful not to use "always" and "never."**

- **Two wrongs make a right**: trying to justify what we did by accusing someone else of doing the same. *e.g. "How can you judge me about being late? I've seen you come in late too."* The actions of the accuser deflect the argument in the discussion. Unfortunately, this type of fallacy has become a standard operating procedure in today's political arena.

These are just a few of the more common fallacies we are likely exposed to on a daily basis. One of the most important tools to combat these fallacies is the **QUESTION**. Don't be reticent to ask for more clarification, examples, evidence that may or may not support one's claim. Being aware of logical fallacies is the first step in dealing with them, and the second step is to confront the fallacy. Confronting fallacious thinking can be a significant challenge for many of us. As I stated earlier in this chapter, collaboration and consensus is usually the most effective way to reach viable decisions. However, that is certainly easier said than done, especially, and ironically, when we value our membership in the group. In 1972, Irving Janis wrote about a group phenomenon called *"Groupthink."* When a group becomes highly cohesive, and members value their membership, they become increasingly susceptible to the Groupthink phenomena, where agreement becomes the norm, possibly leading to poor decisions. Groupthink often occurs when the members' desire for consensus overrides their concerns and desire to present alternatives. Members become reluctant to critique other members' views or to express an unpopular opinion. When this happens, the desire for group cohesion effectively overrides effective decision-making and problem-solving. Janis hypothesized there are eight symptoms of Groupthink to be on the lookout for. As you read about these symptoms, ask yourself if you've experienced any of them in the workplace, at home, and in the various groups that we may participate in outside of work.

Symptoms of Groupthink

Rationalization: This can occur when team members convince themselves that even though evidence is to the contrary, the alternative or decision being presented is the best one. Members may also look at previous decisions that worked before, and rather than critically evaluating the proposed decision, they assume this decision will also work. *"It's always worked before. I'm sure it will this time as well."*

Direct Pressure: When a team member expresses an opposing opinion or questions the rationale behind a decision, one or more of the other members may attempt to overtly or subtley pressure that person into compliance. *"My God, when do you want to launch the new product? Next year?!?"*

Illusion of Invulnerability: After a few successes, the group begins to feel like any decision they make is the right one especially when there is no disagreement from anyone in the group. *"Our track record has been stellar. It speaks for itself."*

Inherent Morality: Each member of the group views him or herself as moral and ethical. After all, everyone wants to do what's right, and they all want a successful outcome. When morality is the basis for decision-making, the pressure to conform is even greater on people to conform. *"We all know what is right, and this is definitely the right thing to do."*

Stereotyping: As the group becomes more insulated from outside views, they begin to see outsiders or even other groups within the same organization as adversaries. These perceived negative characteristics are then used to drive a decision. *"The press will eat us alive if we don't deliver what we said we would."*

Self-Censorship: Members censor their opinions in order to conform because they want to be a "team player," and don't want to be disruptive. *"I'd better not say anything. It will only cause a disruption. Besides, I may be wrong, and it would be embarrassing."*

Mind-Guarding: This is similar to the notion of a "bodyguard" except it is information that is being guarded. Information that's gathered is censored or withheld from the group so that what is available conforms to or supports the chosen decision or alternative. *"We don't have data to corroborate that. I'm sure we have sufficient information to move forward."*

Illusion of Unanimity: This may be the most insidious symptom of all. A closed question may be asked of the entire group, and because no one speaks up, the leader may think the group's decision is unanimous. This is what feeds Groupthink and causes it to spiral out of control. *"Are we all in agreement? Ok, if there are no questions, it's decided then."*

How to Avoid Groupthink

The challenge for any group leader is to help create a working environment in which Groupthink is held to a minimum. It is important also to understand the risks of Groupthink, and to remind ourselves of the symptoms. One way to do this is to list the Groupthink symptoms on the conference room wall in which the team is meeting. This provides a good reminder, and it's a way to warn the group that it may be falling into the Groupthink trap, because it's not always that obvious.

To avoid Groupthink, it's useful to develop a process for checking the assumptions behind important decisions and validate them. The following questions may be useful for validating the process used in making a decision:

- Did we clarify our objectives?

- Did we explore all the alternatives?

- Did we encourage ideas to be challenged without reprisal?

- Did we examine the risks of the preferred choice we made?

- Did we test assumptions?

- If necessary, did we go back and re-examine alternatives that were rejected?

- Did we gather relevant information from outside sources?

- Did we process this information from outside sources objectively?

- Did we develop a contingency plan?

Not only should a team have a process to help avoid Groupthink, it might also have a structure to keep it focused on its goals. Earlier in this chapter, I said that more effective teams utilize a structure and are collaborative. When a team addresses a problem and strives to make a decision to resolve that problem, it usually does better when it solicits input from all of its members and uses a structure that helps them remain focused. The Model on the next page is a 7-step process for addressing a problem and deciding on a decision to resolve it.

7-Step Problem-Solving/Decision-Making Model

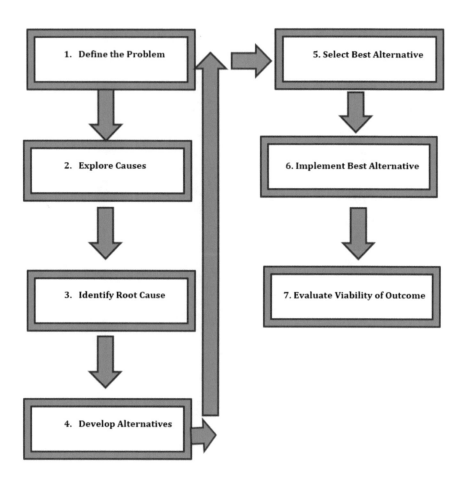

Defining the Problem

The first step of the Model is to define the problem and its cause(s) before developing a solution. This first step is critical because there may be a tendency to assume the problem and prematurely focus on solutions. As I said earlier, if we focus on the solution before we've defined the problem, the solution could **become** the problem. It's often natural to assume what the problem is, but it behooves us to take the time to ensure everyone has defined the problem correctly and is in agreement. Albert Einstein apparently once said that if he only had an hour to save the world, he would spend 55 minutes defining the problem and only 5 minutes solving it. People have different perspectives, interests, and needs which may affect the way they "see" a problem. For example, a manager may define a productivity problem as a function of inefficient, untrained employees, and the employees may see the problem as unrealistic expectations on the part of management, or outdated technology. Parents may see their son or daughter as being too young to attend a particular party, and the son or daughter may see their parents as being unfair and too strict. As I said in a previous chapter, it depends on where the people involved decide to "punctuate" the issue.

There's an exercise I used to do in one of my training classes. I created a hypothetical scenario in which the training participants faced life or death situation. They were asked to rank order from a list, the items most important to their survival. Before they began their group discussion, I would describe the 7-Step Problem-Solving and Decision-Making Model and would ask them to follow it in their discussion. I was often surprised how many times the participants assumed they understood the problem & causes and jumped immediately into ranking the items they believed were most important to their survival. I might add that the participants were usually very bright, well-educated people. Regardless, there seems to be a tendency for many of us to be "solution-focused" instead of "problem-focused", and this tendency can undermine the problem-solving and decision-making process. So, we must always be on guard, and make sure everyone involved has a clear and mutual definition of the problem.

Identifying the Root Cause

Just as we may have difficulty defining the problem, we may also have difficulty identifying the root causes of a problem. A technique that I have found quite useful in identifying root causes is called the "5 Whys." It's a technique used to explore the cause-and-effect relationships underlying a particular problem. The goal is to determine the root cause of a problem by repeating the question "Why?" five times. Sakichi Toyoda, the founder of Toyota Industries developed the 5 Whys technique in the 1930's, and Toyota still uses the technique to solve problems today. The technique seems simple, but one must be careful in its implementation. When a problem occurs, the people closest to the problem sit down and go through the process of drilling down to identify the root cause of the problem by asking "Why" five times. Instead of "solutions," the technique uses the term "counter measures" because the focus is on actions that prevent the problem from happening again, and it's best to use the technique to resolve relatively simple or moderately difficult issues. Let's look at how it might work.

Step 1:

Gather people who are familiar with the problem and describe the process to them. This is important because if you just start asking "why" five times, you will certainly irritate a few people. So let them know what you are doing, and why you are doing it.

Step 2:

Define the problem by writing it out on a flipchart or whiteboard and get everyone's agreement on the definition.

Step 3:

Ask the team why the problem is occurring. Seek answers that are factual instead of unsupported opinions or hearsay. Record the group's succinct responses on the flipchart or whiteboard.

Step 4:

Continue asking "Why" in reference to each answer generated. Stay focused on facts.

Step 5:

You'll begin to have a good idea whether you've identified the root cause of the problem when your "Why" question doesn't generate any more responses. You're not required to ask 5 Whys. You may only need to ask 4 or you might need to ask more than 5. It really is a function of the situation, complexity of the problem, and the group's willingness to candidly approach the issue.

Step 6:

Once you've identified at least one root cause, you need to move to a discussion of counter measures needed to keep the problem from re-occurring.

Step 7:

Be sure to monitor the effectiveness of the counter measures that are implemented. There may be a necessity to amend them or try something else entirely.

Tools to Assist Problem Solving and Decision-Making

Weighted Voting

As I mentioned earlier in this chapter, critical thinking often consists of two types of thinking. The first is Divergent thinking. This is when an individual or group brainstorms all the possible ideas relative to a problem or solution. Once these ideas are laid out visually on paper or a flip chart, the individual or group will move toward Convergent thinking by systematically narrowing the list to the options that appear most viable. The way this might be done is by conducting what is sometimes known as weighted voting. It's a technique that allows for collaboration in a more systematic manner. Let's take an example of how this might be done.

Step 1:

Let's say Jim, the team leader of a large department has a difficult decision to make. Inflation has hit his department with higher prices for labor and materials. His company is not in a position to raise prices, so his department has to come up with a creative solution to rising costs and labor supply while still maintaining a quality product. After clearly explaining the situation to his team, Jim conducts a brainstorming session in which all ideas are solicited and recorded on a flip chart. None of the ideas are evaluated during this "divergent thinking" process. All ideas are acknowledged and recorded on a flip chart.

Step 2:

After the brainstorming session, let's say the team comes up with the following list of 8 options to help resolve the issue:

1. Purchase newer equipment to shorten production time

2. Reduce two administrative staff members

3. Outsource equipment maintenance

4. Outsource janitorial services

5. Reduce subsidized daycare benefits

6. Decrease Break times

7. Temporarily eliminate pay raises for the next 2 years

8. Temporarily eliminate overtime

Step 3:

Make sure everyone understands each of the options and what they would be voting on.

Step 4:

Assign each group member 3 or 4 votes (The number of votes will vary depending on the number of items on the list.)

Step 5:

Each group member is allowed to allocate his or her votes any way they see fit across all of the 8 options. One method of recording votes is to use hash marks or adhesive dots next to each option. For example, if each member has three votes, they can place all of their votes on one option, or they can distribute their votes across the options any way they want.

Step 6:

The remaining items that got the most votes are listed on a flip chart, and the next round of voting begins.

Step 7:

The top two options voted on are listed on the flip chart, and each member has a single vote. The results of this round will represent the group's chosen decision.

Weighted Voting is viewed as a fair, efficient, and inclusive process of group decision- making. It respects and represents everyone's opinions and allows for full participation. It is particularly useful after a brainstorming session when the group has generated many opinions and options. The process is useful when the group needs to narrow their options to a more plausible and viable level.

CT Self-Assessment Tool

This questionnaire will help you identify key areas where your critical thinking and problem-solving skills are strong or could be improved on. Beside each statement, circle the number that best describes how you solve problems and/or make decisions.

1 = Strongly Disagree   2 = Disagree   3 = Uncertain   4 = Agree
5 = Strongly Agree

1. I always ask, "Is this problem worth solving?" before sitting down to solve it.

    1 2 3 4 5

2. I try to break down big problems into manageable pieces---instead of trying to solve the whole problem at once.

    1 2 3 4 5

3. To determine the cause of a problem, I gather enough data to know exactly where, when, and under what circumstances the problem occurs.

    1 2 3 4 5

4. I have a network of contacts with whom I discuss the problems in my area.

    1 2 3 4 5

5. I treat problem solving and decision making as separate processes.

    1 2 3 4 5

6. I usually use problem-solving tools such as brainstorming and/or weighted voting to help me solve problems.

    1 2 3 4 5

7. I involve my team in problem solving when I need team members' help to implement a major decision.

1 2 3 4 5

8. It's impossible to have all the information about a problem before making a decision and taking action.

1 2 3 4 5

9. I involve my team when they know more about a situation than Ido, even though it usually takes longer to get the problem solved.

1 2 3 4 5

10. I usually use brainstorming to generate ideas for problem-solving and decision-making.

1 2 3 4 5

11. My problem solving and decision-making approach balances thoughtful deliberation with an action orientation.

1 2 3 4 5

12. When I have a big problem to solve, I talk to a number of people before coming up with a solution.

1 2 3 4 5

13. Once a solution is implemented, I have a follow-up plan to ensure the solution fixes the problem.

1 2 3 4 5

Interpretation:

13 - 30   Your present problem solving/decision making skills probably have room for improvement.

31 – 50   Your problem solving/decision making skills are probably good, but could be improved.

51 – 65   Your problem solving/decision making skills are probably excellent, with little need for improvement.

To reiterate the theme of this book, for these techniques to work, participants must be clear about what's **expected** of them during the process. It must also be clear that the **intent** of the process is to solve problems and decide on counter measures and improvements. Finally, the process must be collaborative where participants are **acknowledged** for their ideas and contributions. Whether we are working through a difficult situation in our organizational environments, or making personal decisions in our interpersonal lives, critical thinking skills play an important part in our effectiveness in addressing these issues. The ability to define and analyze problems, and avoiding fallacious thinking and cognitive biases, can go a long way in improving our effectiveness at work and at home. Additionally, being systematic and collaborative in resolving issues will help us better analyze information, think more creatively, and help make us more effective managers, supervisors, parents, students, problem-solvers, and decision-makers in whatever life brings to us.

Chapter 5

Nonverbal Communication: It's Not Always What You Say...

Nonverbal Communication

At this point, I'd like to consider some of the basic principles of non-verbal communication, since it permeates all that we do and can dramatically impact our organizational and personal relationships. As I mentioned earlier, others' perceptions of us are often based on what we *don't* say or *how* something was said. Look at the following continuum ranging from zero to one hundred percent. Notice the word "Meaning" above it.

Meaning

0 ↔➤➤➤➤➤➤➤➤➤➤➤➤➤➤➤➤➤◄◄◄◄◄◄◄◄◄◄◄◄◄◄◄◄◄◄◄◄↔100%

When two individuals are talking to each other, how much *meaning* or *interpretation* is based on the *nonverbal* aspects of the interaction? Please keep in mind that I'm not talking about one's understanding of the information. I'm talking about one's *interpretation* of the situation, the issue, or the person, based solely on the nonverbal aspects of the interaction. When people are asked this question in training classes, most say around fifty percent of the meaning is derived from nonverbal behavior. The research suggests different conclusions, especially when there is an **inconsistency** between what people *say* compared with what they *do* nonverbally. According to some research, upwards of eighty percent of the meaning or interpretation of our transactions is derived nonverbally. If there is a disparity between what people *say* and what they *do*, others will tend to believe what they *do*, not what was *said*. We are very much influenced by what someone *does* over what they *say*. To demonstrate this, I sometimes ask training participants to hold up their hands and form an "A-OK" sign. Then I tell them to place the sign on their *chins* while I place the sign on my *cheek*. Invariably, eighty to ninety percent of the participants will place the sign on their *cheeks*. This simple (somewhat corny) exercise shows how we tend to be more influenced by what others *do* rather than what they *say*.

While the nonverbal communication research is quite prolific, for our purposes, let's briefly look at four classifications of nonverbal communication that have particular relevance in our organizational and personal interactions: **kinesics** (body language), **proxemics** (social distance), **paralanguage** (vocal intonation/inflection), and **affect displays** (eyes and facial expressions). All of these nonverbal classifications are somewhat culture dependent. In other words, they may have different degrees of meaning in various cultures. For example, the United States, Canada, Switzerland, and much of Western Europe are referred to in the nonverbal literature as a *low-context* communication cultures. What this means is that much of the information conveyed is mainly from the words that are used instead of the nonverbal aspects of the message. The communication tends to be more direct and straightforward, and relying more on facts rather than intuition and inference in decision-making. The focus tends to be on verbalized detail to maintain clarity in the communication. However, in *high-context* communication cultures, the focus is on implicit and intuitive behaviors, subtley, and context that are known by collective members of that culture. Much of South America, and countries such as Japan, China, and Saudi, Arabia are examples of *high-context* communication cultures where more emphasis is placed on unspoken, subtle communication around context and relationships.

(Kinesics) Body Language: In organizations, our bodies communicate many messages, particularly about our status and interpersonal responsiveness. Generally, in Western culture, individuals who possess a high degree of organizational authority tend to be more expansive and relaxed in the way they act, while individuals of lower organizational authority or status tend to appear more attentive. Sometimes, particularly when a direct report has a concern or problem to discuss, the manager's expansive posture can unintentionally convey a detachment or lack of concern for the other person.

Rule of thumb: when someone expresses concern over a problem or issue, lean slightly forward in your chair, maintain good frontal eye contact, and attend to what is being said by nodding, and/or reinforcing audibly by exhibiting nonverbal acknowledgment.

Managers often underestimate their ability to influence others through their own nonverbal behavior. The behavior we exhibit by our body language can unintentionally or intentionally influence the perception and degree of our empathy toward others. As I mentioned in an earlier chapter, the reality of organizational life is that we tend to judge ourselves by our **INTENTIONS**, but others tend to judge us by our **BEHAVIOR**. No matter what we intend to convey to others, if our nonverbal behavior is inconsistent with what we say verbally, you can bet on it: the other person will believe what is seen, not what is said. (Remember the A-OK exercise cited earlier.)

By way of illustration, when I was a graduate student, I would have periodic, informal discussions with my advisor. During those unscheduled meetings, he had a tendency to tap his foot as he sat at his desk. I found myself cutting off some conversations with him because his foot tapping meant, to me at least, that he didn't have much time to talk, or may be in a hurry to get to other, more pressing matters. Even though he would say, "Come in Ray. What's on your mind?" (foot tapping away!) I felt I was interrupting him from doing more important things. I would often start our conversations by saying, "I know you're busy. I'll only take a minute of your time." Verbally, he always had time for me. However, nonverbally, he didn't. Finally, I mustered up the courage to comment. I said that I knew he was very busy, and since I didn't want to interrupt him, would he prefer that I make an appointment in the future. When he asked what gave me that impression, I nervously said "Well, it's, ah, your foot." He laughed, slapped his knee, and said "I just do that. It's a habit, I guess. Please don't let it bother you." We both laughed, and it became a running joke between us. A question we may ask ourselves, is how many idiosyncratic behaviors or personal habits do we have that could be misinterpreted, and influence others' perceptions of us?

Proxemics (Social Distance): The degree of distance we maintain between each other in our conversations will often define the nature of the relationship. For example, in traditional Western culture, touching to about eighteen inches is usually conducive to intimate relationships, including whispers, secrets, etc. Eighteen inches to about three to four feet is more conducive to personal transactions such as those we have with friends, coworkers, cocktail parties, and social functions. Research in the area of proxemics often categorizes social distance into three zones:

The **intimate zone** is within touching distance, from actually touching to about two feet. The **personal zone** is from two to four feet. The social zone is four to twelve feet apart. The **public zone** is more than twelve feet.

I remember when my wife and I first moved to the Washington, DC area, we attended a social function at one of the DC hotels. I was standing in the middle of a large ballroom, talking to a man from Saudi, Arabia. He spoke very rapidly, and in the classic Seinfeld tradition (which won't make any sense unless you are a Seinfeld fan), stood very close to me while talking. He was a "close talker" and certainly within the personal zone, which was inconsistent with what I considered comfortable. I found myself nodding a great deal, while backing up a little at a time—until he backed me up against the wall! He was invading my personal zone, and I was trying to compensate by trying to expand the distance toward the social zone where I felt much more comfortable. Finally, I smiled, and said, "Excuse me, but I'm having a really difficult time talking this close." He responded by laughing and explaining that in his culture, the "feeling of one's breath on one's face is a sign of a good relationship." I smiled back, saying "That's really interesting," and quickly considered offering him a breath mint.

Much of the research on social distance may be re-evaluated since the outbreak of COVID-19, but we can see from the above example, social distance, and much of non-verbal behavior tend to be culture dependent. However, we can generally conclude that regardless of the culture, and new standards of social distancing, people tend to do two things when they feel their personal space is invaded: (1) People tend to maximize the tolerable distance between them, and (2) They tend to minimize the degree of eye contact (notice this the next time you get into an elevator with one other person who's a stranger).

Proxemics also pertains to the way we arrange our furniture, and where we sit during certain transactions. For example, the desk and chair arrangement can affect a transaction. Sitting across from one another with a desk between you and the other person tends to be more conducive to formal and possibly competitive transactions; sitting side-by-side, or at right angles tends to be more conducive to informal, cooperative transactions. People also tend to feel more at ease and collaborate more when they sit this way than they do sitting face-to-face (eyeball to eyeball) across a table. If you are fortunate enough at work to have an office instead of a cubicle, how does the seating arrangement look? Do you feel it helps or hinders the kinds of transactions you want to occur? On a personal note, when we bought our first house in Maryland, we had three young, growing boys. The kitchen had a countertop instead of a table to sit at. Maybe because I'm Italian, and grew up in a loving Italian household, I believe in the importance of eating together with the family whenever possible, but sitting at the counter made me feel like we were sitting at the local "diner." We were all looking straight ahead, rather than at each other, and my wife and I thought it reduced our interaction with one another. Within 3 months of moving in, we had the countertop removed, made a few other modifications, and bought a round kitchen table large enough for all of us to sit down to eat and talk together. In my opinion, it made a big difference in the quality of our interactions with one another.

Rule of thumb: At work, if you want to "formalize" a transaction such as a discipline or employment interview, you may want to sit face-to-face with your desk between you and the other person. If you want to de-formalize a transaction, and you want to increase the tendency to be more cooperative and collaborative, sit around a table or at right angles to one another.

Paralanguage (vocal inflection & intonation): There's a good deal of truth in the statement, "It's not always what we say, but how we say it." The tone, volume, and pitch of a person's voice can significantly influence the "meaning" of the message. While we can often control the words we choose to use, it's often not as easy to control the way in which the

words are spoken. Pauses, intonation, volume, and so forth, express our feelings much more clearly than the words themselves. The interesting thing is that in situations where we have strong feelings about something, we tend to be less capable of masking the paralinguistic elements of our words. Additionally, others will tend to believe the paralinguistic part of the message over the verbalized message. Here's a little exercise to try to make this point. Speaking in a monotone voice, say the following: **"I didn't say he stole the book."** Now repeat the sentence, but this time emphasize the word **"I."** The listener may conclude that someone else may have said he stole the book, but not *you*. Repeat the sentence again, but this time, emphasize the word **"say."** The listener may now conclude that you might have *alluded* to him stealing the book, but you didn't actually say it. Repeat the sentence again, but this time, emphasize the word **"he."** Now the listener may conclude that *someone else* may have stolen the book, but not him. Stick with me, here. Repeat the sentence again, but this time, emphasize the word **"stole."** Now the listener may conclude that he didn't steal the book, but he may have *borrowed* it. Finally, repeat the sentence again, but this time, emphasize the word **"book."** Now the listener may conclude that he may have stolen the car—but he didn't steal that book! (Another corny example, but I hope the point was made.)

By changing the emphasis and inflection of a single word, the entire meaning of what is said can change for the other person. Additionally, we may not even be aware of it, especially when the situation is an emotional one. One of the reasons people may be so sensitive to paralanguage is that we probably learned it in the crib! At a pre-verbal state, while in the crib, we heard those adult voices "oohing" and "ahhing." Our inherent "fight or flight" tendencies were affected by the vocal intonations and inflections from those adults around the crib. As adults, if we talked in our normal tone of voice, we might scare the child, and trigger more of a "flight" response. Consequently, as humans, we are probably pretty good at distinguishing variations in the paralanguage of another person, because that's how we began to make sense out of our world—in the crib!

Rule of thumb: When there is a disparity between what we say and how we say it, people will tend to believe *how* we say it over *what* we say.

Affect Displays (facial expressions and eye contact): We all know that our facial expressions can affect our transactions with others. Generally speaking, the research has identified seven emotions displayed by our facial expressions. They are sadness, anger, disgust, fear, interest, surprise and happiness. These emotions are normally conveyed through our facial expressions, and we often have little control over them. It's not as easy as we might think to hide these seven emotions. One must make a conscious effort to do so, and even then, they will tend to show through sometime during a transaction. If you want to pursue this topic further, go to "Dr. Google," and take a look at the Leathers Facial Meaning Sensitivity Test (FMST). It asks the test taker to look at ten photos with various facial expressions representing disgust, anger, fear, sadness, happiness, surprise and contempt, and match the emotion being conveyed in each photo. It's an interesting way to evaluate your own nonverbal sensitivity.

Another affect display is eye contact. Referred to as the "windows to the soul" by Shakespeare, eye contact can be both revealing and deceiving. Let's take a look at just a few of the research conclusions regarding eye contact (Goldhaber, 1979):

1. Eye contact seems to occur more under the following conditions:

   b. When people seek feedback from others

   c. When people want to signal a need for involvement or inclusion

   d. When people want to signal a need for affection

   e. When people want to exhibit aggression toward others

2. Eye contact seems to occur less under the following conditions:

   a. When people want to hide their inner feelings; feel uncomfortable, embarrassed, etc.

   b. When two people are physically close to one another

   c. When people dislike one another, or after recent deception

   d. When people begin a long utterance, or when the listener anticipates a long, boring utterance.

e. When people want to discontinue maintaining social contact.

Generally, we tend to respond to positive nonverbal feedback by looking more at that person, and looking less at people who don't give us any overt nonverbal feedback. I remember when I was working on my PhD, a fellow student and good friend, asked if he could have a copy of a paper I had presented at a conference. He appealed to my ego by saying he wanted to cite my paper in some research he was doing. I was flattered by his request, but told him I was on my way to teach a class, and I didn't want to be late. He said if it was that important to me, he would start my class for me while I got him the paper he requested. I agreed and went to my office to get him the research paper while he convened my class. Little did I know, before I got to the classroom, my friend had told the students on the left side of the room to give me "positive" feedback during my lecture/discussion, and for the right side of the room to give me "negative" feedback by looking bored and uninterested. I hate to admit it, but sometimes, I just don't get things very quickly. While speaking to the class, I found myself on the left side of the room. Students were nodding their heads, maintaining great eye contact, and generally exhibiting overall positive "A" behaviors. Periodically, I'd go to the right side of the room, and students were providing very little eye contact, looking out the window, doodling, scratching, and exhibiting overall negative "F" behaviors. Consequently, I tended to go back to the left side of the room where I felt much more comfortable. Finally, in the front row of the right side of the room, one of my best students was sleeping! I walked over and nudged his elbow, and said "Come on man, wake up. Am I that boring?" At that point, everyone started laughing. I felt like a complete idiot, with no other alternative but to laugh at myself as well. I was being manipulated and responding to the type of nonverbal feedback I was receiving and didn't even realize it. As I said, sometimes I just don't get things very quickly.

One more example. I have a good friend who is a retired detective from New York City, and he's seen it all. One day after a round of golf together, we were sharing "war stories" of our work with law enforcement officers. He worked in homicide and had many stories about his experiences, and over the years, in my training and consulting business, I had conducted training for nearly 1,000 law enforcement officers. He had a very interesting nonverbal observation of people who were arrested and placed in a holding room until they were to be interrogated for a crime that was committed. Through a one-way mirror, detectives would observe the nonverbal behavior of the suspects in the holding room. The ones that showed a significant amount of nervousness were surprisingly not always guilty, and according to my friend who had a great deal of experience in this sort of thing, found that the one thing the more guilty suspects tended to do was---fall asleep!! That's right, the guilty ones tended to fall asleep in the holding room prior to, and after interrogation. So, observing nonverbal behavior may tell you only part of the story, and it may not be what you think.

I want to provide a general word of caution before concluding this section on nonverbal communication. Don't attempt to overly interpret nonverbal behavior independent of the social and verbal context. They are interrelated. So, the next time, someone crosses his/her arms during a conversation, don't draw any conclusions until you've considered the social context, the relationship, and the message being conveyed. After all, the person could simply be more comfortable that way.

Some of the more interesting areas of research in nonverbal communication center on the following areas:

- The increased use of digital communication tools such as emojis, gifs (Graphics Interchange Format), and video conferencing applications such as Zoom that can convey emotions and reactions.

- Cross-cultural similarities and differences research is even more important as we live in a more globalized world.

- The impact of the significant advances in artificial intelligence and facial recognition software may lead to a greater understanding of facial expressions and emotions.

- Technology is allowing for more research and a better understanding of micro-expressions, eye movements and various physiological behaviors.

- Nonverbal communication in healthcare, and the way providers convey information to patients, and its impact on outcomes and patient satisfaction.

- Nonverbal communication in education, especially virtual learning platforms, and ways to facilitate learning and engagement.

- The impact of how certain nonverbal behaviors convey power and dominance or submissiveness, especially in the workplace, and in politics.

- Research is presently being conducted to develop artificial intelligence (AI) systems that can interpret and generate nonverbal cues to enhance interactions between humans and computers. It's a brave new world out there!!

Chapter 6

Managing Expectations Through Effective Feedback

Or - "You have a minute? I'd like to talk."

Virtually everyone wants to be successful and excel in his/her work and personal life. A great deal of pride, satisfaction and self-esteem can be derived from doing something well, and it's extremely gratifying to receive positive feedback about our accomplishments. Armed with a clear understanding of what is expected, I believe most people will rise to the challenge of greater productivity and effectiveness. Success in the productivity realm, therefore, hinges on management deciding what it expects employees to accomplish, communicating this in a clear, direct manner, and providing opportunities for employee questions and feedback. However, these types of conversations can be challenging at times, because people often don't know how to give effective feedback. If managers give only positive feedback, regardless of how well the employee actually did the job, things could backfire. Sometimes, managers may want to be "liked," so they give only positive feedback, or they think that "democratic" leaders only are supposed to give positive feedback to create a more motivating environment. Both of those views can potentially create an unhealthy and unproductive work environment.

As I briefly mentioned in another chapter, there are two potential problems that can occur when an employee only receives positive feedback, even when their performance was less than effective. First, they usually know when they've not done as well as they could or should have. So, when the manager says they did a "great job," it may well undermine the manager's credibility because the employees know the manager isn't being truthful or is just being naïve. Secondly, employees may begin to believe that they are doing a "great job" even when they are not. This could create a distorted view of their own effectiveness, leading to potentially difficult performance discussions for both parties.

People want and expect honesty in their relationships. Effective managers understand that if an employee does a good job, specific, positive feedback should be provided to the employee. However, if an employee doesn't do such a great job, effective managers understand that their responsibility is to coach the employee, and provide specific, constructive performance feedback.

Usually, positive feedback tends to embellish the behavior, so people will usually continue that behavior in which they receive the positive feedback. However, the only way someone will actually change the behavior is when the feedback is constructive, not just positive. As I said before, some managers want to be liked, or are concerned about hurting the employee's feelings, or they think a good leader should only give positive feedback, or more importantly, they don't really know *how* to give constructive feedback. Consequently, they just provide positive feedback, leading to other problems down the road.

I'm an avid golfer, but not a very good one--I'm sorry to say. If I take golf lessons to improve my game, and no matter how I hit the ball, the golf pro tells me I'm doing a "great job," I will probably get really good at doing something badly! The only way I can improve in this situation is for the golf pro to provide me with feedback on what I'm doing well so I can continue to do that, and what I need to do differently to improve my game. The golf pro must provide me with positive feedback so I can continue to do certain things well, and constructive feedback so I can improve. It doesn't matter if you're a manager, team leader, supervisor, individual contributor, parent, or golf pro. Knowing how to effectively give and receive constructive feedback is a necessary part of our roles.

This notion of only providing positive feedback has even been manifested by our school systems where everyone is a "winner," and there are no "losers." I realize I've said this before, but the focus on feelings over learning essentials is not a good educational path to be on. So, not to hurt anyone's feelings, everyone gets a trophy. In my opinion, this leads to children growing up not experiencing failure. This tends to lead to an inability to deal effectively with adversity or things that don't go well. This can make it difficult to receive constructive feedback from others, because they have grown up being told they are winners and "special." Unfortunately, life isn't that way. The reality is that failure is sometimes a part of life, and not experiencing it can potentially lead to a good deal of narcissistic thinking, making it difficult to receive or give constructive feedback when it's necessary. Not knowing how to *give or receive* constructive feedback can lead to significant problems in every relationship.

The same thing applies to parenting. If a child only receives positive feedback, even when they do something wrong or ineffectively, the parent is not doing them any favors by ignoring it because they don't want to hurt their child's feelings, or because they want to be "liked," or they simply *don't know how to give constructive feedback.* A parent's job is to always be loving and supportive, but also to provide constructive feedback which nurtures, coaches and teaches their children how to improve and make better choices.

A number of years ago, I had a discussion with a neighbor about parenting. He was telling me that he believed that a good parent should also be their children's best friend and "buddy." I acknowledged what he said, and I told him that I saw it differently. I said that I didn't want to be my children's buddy or best friend. I needed to be their parent, and that my job was to be clear and fair about the rules, and my expectations about what was right and wrong, and that some things were simply not okay **(Expectations)**.

I also said that as a parent, I always needed to show that I love and support them **(Acknowledgment)** and I always have their best interest in mind **(Intentions)**. I also remember telling him that children need to understand the nature of consequences, and that if there are no consequences, then why should they change their behavior that may be unacceptable? For that matter, in the work environment, if there are no consequences for poor performance, then why should the employee change?

Problem "Ownership"

A few years ago, I was doing some consulting and training work for a large insurance company in Manhattan. Their corporate headquarters building was on Sixth Avenue. For a number of business reasons, the company decided to move part of its operation to New Jersey. Anyone who has either lived or visited that area has probably dealt with traffic, bridges, trains, and crowds. It can sometimes be a bit challenging. Pete, one of the employees that needed to move to New Jersey, had been coming late to work nearly every day since the move, and it affected the team in many ways. A number of other team members complained about Pete's tardiness. Consequently, Eadie, who was Pete's supervisor, also became concerned about Pete's lateness.

Eadie normally held a team meeting every morning. At these meetings, she provided up-dates and assigned various tasks and requirements for the day. Pete's lateness required her to go back and reassign some tasks. This became inefficient, and quite frankly, irritating for Eadie and her team. Eadie decided to hold a meeting with Pete to discuss his lateness.

At the meeting, Eadie told Pete he'd been late quite often, but didn't provide him with any documentation. Pete denied he'd been late and asked for proof. Eadie became defensive and said that Pete "had a problem" ever since a portion of the company made the move to New Jersey. Pete denied that he had a problem. He reacted by saying it was Eadie who had the problem, and in fact, thought he'd been doing fine. The meeting ended badly, with both parties feeling angry and defensive.

If you were in Eadie's place, what would you decide to do and how would you do it? Before you answer that, please ask yourself this question: "Who "owns" this problem?" Does Pete "own" it, or does Eadie "own" this problem? It may seem like an obvious question with an obvious answer. Sometimes, I present a video of this scenario in a training session, and then ask the question "Who owns the problem?" I tell training participants they can't say both own the problem. I ask them to choose either Pete or Eadie and the rationale for their choice. It's interesting how often participants would say Pete owns the problem because after all, he's the one who's coming in late, and it's his responsibility to be on time. Others often say that Eadie owns the problem because she's Pete's supervisor, and it's her responsibility, or because she didn't provide documentation, or didn't communicate very effectively. All of that may be true, but the best way to determine the important question of "who owns the problem?" is to ask *who's the one **concerned** about it?* If you ask Pete if there's a problem with his lateness, he will likely say *no*. If you ask Eadie if there's a problem with Pete's lateness, I'm pretty sure she will say *yes*.

Remember this, folks. **The person who owns the problem is the one who's concerned about it!** Eadie's job is to make her **intentions** clear, and to ask for Pete's help and cooperation. She must know how to more effectively provide specific, documented feedback. She must actively listen and **acknowledge** what Pete has to say. She must be clear about her **expectations**, and she must be prepared to discuss consequences if necessary. That's a long list of things she needs to do. Eadie's job is to effectively transfer the ownership of the problem from her to Pete. Understanding who "owns" the problem can help us understand how to communicate more effectively with the other person.

Here's a little rule: If the *other person* "owns" the problem, it means they have a particular concern about something. In that situation, you want to acknowledge the person's concern by actively listening, while practicing good nonverbals such as nodding, eye contact, and attending to them with your body language.

However, if *you* "own" the problem, you want to use specific, nonjudgmental, descriptive language, and follow a structured way of presenting your views. Knowing who "owns" the problem can be very useful in deciding what and when specific skills should be used in the interaction. This knowledge can act as a rule to determine the appropriate skills to use during a difficult conversation.

The "hard" sciences such as mathematics, physics, and chemistry, have predictable rules and formulas. However, in the "soft" science of communication, there are few rules and formulas that are predictable. I like the notion of "problem ownership" because it provides some rules that can help us predict the best way to approach situations that are fluid and dynamic. Let's take a look at these skills more specifically.

Judgmental and Descriptive Language

As I said, when *you* own the problem you need to approach the other person respectfully, using specific nonjudgmental, descriptive language, and follow a structured way of presenting your views. Nonjudgmental, descriptive language describes behavior. It doesn't infer a judgment about that behavior. Below is a list of the characteristic differences between judgmental and descriptive language.

Characteristics of "Judgmental" and "Descriptive" Language

The language used can determine the effectiveness of your feedback

(When giving someone feedback when you own the problem, which type of language do you use?)

Judgmental Language	Descriptive Language
Tells about your reaction ("I'm upset with you...")	Tells about events and behaviors
Isn't observed or verified	Is observed and verified
Uses You Messages such as "You need to be..., You should..., You'd better, ought to..."	Uses I Messages such as "I want, I need, I would appreciate, I would like..."
Uses "allness" terms, or as if something is absolute. (always, never)	Includes qualifiers in terms of time, extent, circumstances. "From my perspective, this is how I see it..."
General/Abstract	Specific/Concrete
Evaluative & Judgmental. Focuses on the person's attitudes	Relatively free of judgment. Focuses on behavior- not the person
Assumes and Attributes motives to behavior	Doesn't attribute motives. Asks person for motive

Results:	Results:
Agreement is difficult Defensiveness is high	Can gain agreement easier Defensiveness is minimized

I think it's safe to assume that descriptive language is much more effective than judgmental language. If we were on the receiving end of it, we would much prefer the other person not use terms that are judgmental and use more descriptive terms in their communication. Even though it's obvious to us that descriptive language is preferred, the reality of life is that it's very likely that we grew up hearing judgmental language from significant other people in our lives. Unfortunately, it is more natural. In fact, I will go so far as to say, that in order to be an effective communicator, one must learn to do *unnatural* things. Descriptive language is not natural. It must be learned and practiced, and in everyday encounters, is not always easy to master.

As I said, it's important to use descriptive language, and use it in a structured way—but how? One of the best tools to use when giving effective feedback when *you* own the problem is the **SBIS** Model. It's a structured way of providing feedback to someone when *you* have the concern. Let's take a closer look at it.

SBIS Model

Situation

Describe the situation you are concerned about. It may be a project, process, decision, etc. It's extremely important that you don't focus on the person by focusing on their attitudes, motives, etc. Focus on the situation by *describing* it.

Behavior

What is the person doing or not doing in this situation? Describe-Don't Judge. Again, it's extremely important to describe the behavior and not judge it. This is much more difficult to do than one might think. That's why it's so important to use descriptive rather than judgmental language.

Impact

What is the *Impact* of the person's behavior on the situation? Again, focus on the impact of the behavior (e.g. It's the **lateness-** not Pete)**. Sometimes, it's surprising how often people are essentially unaware of how their behavior may impact others. (Remember the team leader who didn't say good morning?)

Specify

Specify what you need or want from the person--Keep it Future-Oriented! Do not get hung up talking about the past or previous discussions. Try to focus on what can be done from this point forward, and what the other person might do to remedy the situation. If possible, ask the other person to come up with ways to resolve the issue, because then they "own" it.

The **SBIS** Model is a systematic way of providing feedback to someone in a descriptive and helpful manner. Let's take a closer look at the way it might have worked in the situation with Pete and Eadie. This is what it might sound like.

Situation

Eadie: Hi, Pete. Thanks for taking the time to meet with me today.

Pete: Sure.

Eadie: Pete, as you know, since we moved part of our operation to New Jersey, a number of people have been having difficulty getting to work on time.

Pete: I know. It's been difficult for a lot of us.

Behavior

Eadie: I agree. I've noticed that you've been late quite often in the last couple weeks.

Pete: I disagree. I know I've been late a couple times, but it's not a problem.

Eadie: I understand that you and the other team members have been extremely dependable, but this New Jersey move has been difficult for most of us. Let me show you something (shows Pete the documentation). As you can see, the documentation shows that you've been late six times in the last two weeks. What do you think is causing this lateness?

Pete: I don't know. I really don't think it's such a big deal.

Impact

Eadie: I understand. Let me explain the impact the lateness (not Pete) has on the team and me. As you know, every morning, we have our team meeting where I make the assignments for that day, and deal with any issues that come up. If you're not there, and come in late, I then need to make changes and reassign people for that day. At times this has had a big impact on our team's and my efficiency. Do you see why this has become a problem for me?

Pete: I guess. I didn't realize my lateness was that big a deal. I'll tell you though, the traffic has been a major problem for me getting in here on time.

Specify

Eadie: I appreciate that, Pete. Now that you're aware of why it's important that I need to have you here on time for the morning meetings, what do you think you need to do differently?

Pete: Well, I'll just have to try harder to get here on time.

Eadie: Thanks Pete. I appreciate that. What do you think you can do to make that happen?

Pete: I guess I can set my alarm for a half hour earlier. That should get me here for the morning meetings.

Eadie: That's great, Pete. Do you think that will solve it for us?

Pete: I think so. I once went to a week-long training session, and if you were late the instructor would lock you out. I set my alarm for 30 minutes earlier, and I wasn't late once.

Eadie: (Smiles). That was some hard-nosed instructor! Thanks, Pete. I appreciate your understanding and willingness to work with me on this. See you at tomorrow's meeting.

A few things need to be mentioned here. Please remember that this process is a *dialogue*, not a monologue. Between and within each of the steps, you want to listen closely to the other person, ask questions for more information and clarification. In other words, not only must you be clear, specific, and descriptive in your language, you must also actively listen to the other person. Additionally, recognize that it may not always work for you. However, following this structure puts you in a much better position to be successful, with mutual benefit being the result.

It's important that once you identify the situation, describe the person's behavior and impact in that situation, you stay focused on the *future*. Too many of these types of discussions fall into the trap of focusing on the past. When you focus on the past, and don't have data to support your views, you have to depend on your memory and/or your perceptions, and in my case, both of those are fragile! So, don't focus on the past. I'll tell you something about the past. It's over! You can't control it. So, why would anyone want to spend so much time and energy on something that can no longer be controlled? The only thing you may have any control over is the future. Don't get sucked into talking about the past. You can certainly use the past as a frame of reference, but focus more on the future, and what you and the other person can and will do differently.

Now that you have a tool that will help you provide feedback to someone when *you* have a concern (you own the problem), what should you do when the *other* person has the concern (he or she owns the problem)? This is when you are an *active listener*. Let's take a closer look at what active listening actually means.

Active Listening

For me at least, the term "Active Listening" essentially means that you take an active part in the dialogue with the other person by practicing the following important skills:

Paraphrasing: Putting in your own words, the *content* of what the other person is saying. Paraphrasing helps us clarify and verify our understanding of the other person's concerns, positions and views. When you paraphrase content, you might say "Let me see if I understand....," or "If I understand correctly, you want to....," or "Before we conclude, I'd like to summarize my understanding of...." Paraphrasing is important because it helps to clarify and verify information and your understanding of it. It is also a subtle form of **acknowledgment** by showing the other person you respect their views by trying to understand them. It is such an important skill that I don't think anyone can truly be an effective listener if it's not done. It is an inherent part of effective listening, which needs to be practiced, because it's not always a natural way of responding for many people, because as I said in a previous chapter, we have a natural tendency to focus on solutions.

The military often refers to paraphrasing as a "back brief," and it's a skill used when a person is given a task to perform. In this situation, the person responsible for carrying out the task "briefs it back" to his or her officer to clarify and verify understanding of the tasking.

In my opinion, you want to be careful not to use paraphrasing clichés such as "What I hear you say....," or "What I'm hearing is...." I'm not saying they are wrong, but I think they have become somewhat cliché and can be perceived as less than genuine. These phrases sound like you just learned them in some training class, and you now want to try them out on someone. If it's not genuine, it will show. You're better off simply saying "Let me see if I understand...."

Reflecting: Putting in your own words, your understanding and **acknowledgment** of the other person's *feelings*. It is a form of paraphrasing. However, it focuses more on the person's feelings rather than the content of their message. Reflecting helps us to validate, clarify, verify, and better understand the overt and underlying feelings the other person may have about an issue or concern. When you reflect feelings, you might say "It sounds like you feel...," or "It must be very frustrating for you...." Reflecting feelings is important because it affirms the feelings of others. When people sense their feelings are being heard and validated, they tend to be much more open and honest in their communication.

Think about a time when you and another person had a conflict or a misunderstanding of some sort, and you decide to sit down with the person to resolve it. However, as you discuss the issue, the other person tells you that you're "overreacting," or that you shouldn't feel the way you do, or that you're making a big issue out of nothing. My guess is the discussion went downhill from there, and the issue may have even gotten worse. When someone is told they shouldn't feel the way they do, it becomes difficult to move forward because the person's feelings are being discounted and de-valued. In other words, they are not being **acknowledged.** It's important not to tell someone how they "should" feel, or to tell the person not to feel a certain way. We may not agree with the other person's feelings, but it's important that we let the person know that we are making an effort to understand them. After all it's their feelings, not ours. Again, reflecting feelings must be genuine. As with paraphrasing, it is a skill, not a tool to manipulate.

Probing: Probing consists of asking a combination of **closed, open**, and **clarifying** questions in order to better understand or clarify something. They can also be used to gather more information and to help direct the conversation.

Closed questions are usually ones that can be answered with a one-word response such as *yes* or *no*. Generally, closed questions don't provide much new information. An example of a closed question is "Are you satisfied with your job?"

Open questions are usually ones that cannot be answered with a single word response. The person has to say something other than yes or no. Open questions usually provide us with more information and detail. They can also be used to redirect the conversation and provide us with more information about the issues being discussed. An example of an open question is "What aspects of your job do you find most satisfying?"

Clarifying questions can be both open and closed. Their primary function is to clarify a situation, issue, and information. An example of a clarifying question might be "I'm not sure what you mean. Could you give an example?"

Let me give you a short example of how the use of appropriate questions and paraphrasing can lead to better understanding. Over the years, my training and consulting work with the U.S. Navy and other Defense Department agencies, required me to make numerous trips to Guam and Japan. A number of years ago, during my first trip to Guam, I was giving some instructions to a person who spoke English as a second language. As I gave him information regarding what I needed done, he responded with numerous head nods, often saying "Okay" and "No problem." After giving him the instructions, I asked him if he had any questions, and his immediate response was "No problem." Unfortunately, there was a problem, because he didn't understand. Sometimes people think they do understand something, but actually don't. Another possibility is they may not want to admit they don't understand because it would be embarrassing for them to admit it. In this case, it could have also been part of the person's culture not to "disagree" out of respect for the other person. Regardless, I look back on that incident, and realize that it was really *my* ineffective use of listening skills that caused the misunderstanding. First of all, I asked a closed question ("Do you have any questions?"). Secondly, his answer, "No problem," didn't really tell me what he actually understood, and I mistakenly assumed understanding. Third, I made the mistake of not asking him to "back brief" the instructions for me to confirm his understanding. The way to do that was to put the responsibility on myself for being *clear*, and not put the responsibility on the other person for *understanding*. In this case, I might have said something like this. "I just want to make sure I've been clear. What are the steps you plan to take to get this done? I just want to make sure how we're going to proceed..." It's important to place emphasis on *our clarity* rather than emphasis on *the other person's understanding*. When we focus on the latter, it usually makes people feel they are being "tested," and when people feel they are being tested, they feel they are being judged. When they feel they are being judged, they tend to become defensive. When they become defensive, they tend to stop listening. Now, whenever I hear someone say, "No problem," I'm reminded of that incident.

An active listener tries not to criticize, judge the other person, or give advice. The goal of active listening is to clarify your understanding of what the other person is saying, and how they feel about it. These are the primary skills to use when the other person "owns" the problem. They help you get a better understanding of those concerns.

Here's an example of an exercise my wife and I have been doing for many years, and it has been helpful. If either one of us (Person A and Person B) has a concern (owns the problem), we take some time to sit down and do the following:

Listening Exercise

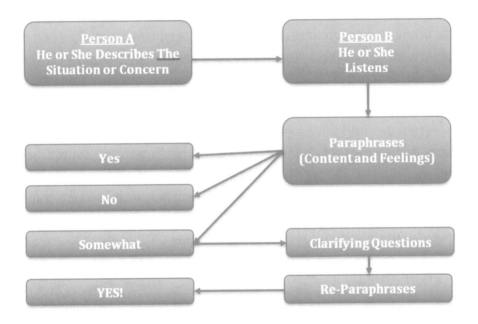

Person A describes an issue of concern. Person B listens without interruption, and then paraphrases his or her understanding of the concern and how Person A likely feels about it. This is where it gets a bit challenging. After Person B paraphrases, Person A can only answer by saying **Yes** (Person B has complete understanding), **No** (complete misunderstanding), or **Somewhat** if Person B exhibited understanding but left out some relevant details.

If Person B receives a **Yes**, the two parties begin exploring ways to resolve the issue. If Person B receives a **No** or **Somewhat,** Person B must ask a series of **clarifying questions**. At this stage, Person A continues to give the one-word answers until Person B is ready to re-paraphrase, and gets a **Yes** response from Person A. When

Person B receives a **Yes** response, both parties fundamentally agree on the concern and may be in a better position to resolve it. Unless both parties define the issue or concern in a mutually acceptable way, it will become very difficult to resolve it.

One other thing. When Person B receives a **Yes,** before attempting to resolve the issue, it's important for Person B to **acknowledge** the other person's concern. Person B doesn't necessarily need to agree with it, but the acknowledgment validates Person A's right to have the concern. This exhibits empathy, which can go a long way in helping to resolve the issue.

My wife and I have been doing this little exercise for years, and it has been extremely helpful. It can also be frustrating sometimes, because it's not always as easy as it might seem. However, I think it's certainly worth the effort. As I said earlier, it doesn't do much good to tell people how they *should feel*, but it certainly is helpful to know, understand and respect those feelings. After all, who am I to tell anyone how he or she is supposed to feel? All I can do is make an effort to understand.

In **Appendix A**, there's a short exercise you can do to assess your own listening skills.

Chapter 7

Responding to Mistakes: The Destructive Force of "Blame"

For many years, we've lived in the Washington, DC, area, which in my opinion, is the center of the "Blame Culture." In recent years, we've seen back-to-back investigations and efforts to ruin the lives of decent people and their families. However, we've also seen executives from a large Gulf oil spill refusing to accept responsibility by attempting to shift the blame to others. Personally, I have little respect for most of our lawmakers in both the Senate and the House, but that criticism is for another time. I don't want to be guilty of the same thing I intend to argue against, which is the unfortunate human frailty of the "blame game." While blame seems to be a natural human tendency, it is also one of the most destructive forces in all organizational and interpersonal relationships. The tendency to blame others will undermine the very fabric of relationships, teams, organizations, and families. It simply doesn't work!

A Harvard Business Review article shows that people who play the "blame game" by blaming others for their own mistakes tend to lose status and credibility, and are poorer performers compared to people who are willing to own up to their mistakes. Additionally, teams and organizations that have a "culture of blame" tend to be less creative and innovative and much less willing to take risks. After all, who wants to be blamed if the risk taken doesn't work out?

Another problem with blame is that it's contagious. When one person, especially the manager, attributes blame, the behavior becomes psychologically validated. This validation that it's okay to blame others tends to permeate throughout the team or organizational culture. That's why it's so important that the manager or leader sets the tone that blame is not an acceptable behavior, and people must feel psychologically safe to own up to their own mistakes. However, it's easier said than done. Blame is so much a part of us. For example, when we were children, think about the number of times we might have blamed our brothers, sisters, friends, or parents when things didn't go our way, or when we were afraid of being disciplined. Actually, people may get more "training" in blaming others than having to own up to their mistakes and actions.

That's why leaders must create a psychologically safe organizational culture by making their **Intentions** clear, that blame is an unacceptable behavior that will not be tolerated; creating the **Expectations** of a responsible culture, where everyone is responsible for what they think, feel and do; and **Acknowledging** people for owning up to their mistakes, with a willingness to explore solutions.

Let's take a closer look at the psychological chain reaction that occurs when someone is blamed for a mistake. In doing that, I want to cite Chuck Swindall, a minister I respect a great deal. He makes the relevant point that "Ten percent of our lives is what happens to us, but ninety percent is how we **respond.**" Things happen to all of us in our lives, but it's how we *respond* to those things that makes the difference. So, how do *you* tend to respond to mistakes? I want you to think about that a bit. When someone makes a mistake, how do you tend to respond? Do you tend to blame the person for the mistake, or do you try to find out what happened, what was learned from it, and then mutually seek a resolution? My observation is that people may do the latter more often at work than they do at home or in their interpersonal lives. I think part of the reason for this is that at work, people have guidelines, rules, hierarchy, structure, defined roles, and of course, consequences for their behavior. However, at home, those rules often go out the window. There are fewer guidelines, rules, hierarchy, structure, defined roles, and consequences in families and interpersonal relationships. So, people may respond differently, and maybe at times, less effectively. It's ironic in that we have to be very careful not to create a culture of blame with the people we care the most about.

In order to understand the significance of blame's impact on organizational relationships, let's take a look at the following scenario.

Scenario

A manager has an employee with a good deal of experience. Let's call the employee Jim. There's an important project that needs to be completed with an internal customer, so the manager decides to give Jim the reins to handle the project and take it to completion. The manager feels that Jim has the necessary technical experience, and has a good rapport with internal customers, so he tells Jim to deal directly with the customer. The manager says he wants Jim to do whatever he thinks is necessary to complete the project in a timely fashion, and Jim is pleased that the manager trusts him to handle it. He appreciates the opportunity to be empowered to do what he thinks is necessary to accomplish what needs to be done.

Things were going well for about a week until Jim made a decision that didn't turn out well. In fact, it turned out to be a big problem. The manager is extremely upset, and calls Jim into his office. Without asking Jim for his assessment of the situation, the manager says "I can't believe you did this! Do you realize the dilemma you've put me in? You can't just go off and make those kinds of decisions without checking with me first! How am I going to explain this to my boss now?" Jim says "I know it didn't work out, but it wasn't all my fault. You told me I was empowered to handle the situation the way I saw fit, but you didn't give me enough instructions! Besides, it wasn't all my fault. Why are you just blaming me?" The manager responds by saying "Yes, you were empowered to handle the project, but I didn't tell you to be stupid about it!" At that point, Jim becomes visibly upset and storms out of the office.

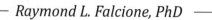

Let's take a closer look at how this situation represents a vicious cycle of blame. The following model represents how it plays out. In fact, we can call it the "Blame Cycle."

Blame Cycle

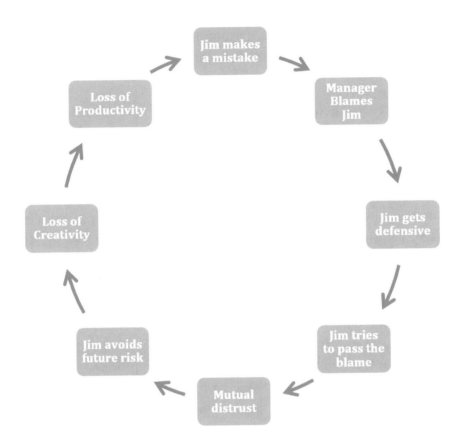

Unfortunately, the above cycle is played out every day in organizations, families and other interpersonal relationships. I would guess that all of us have either observed or experienced it sometime during our careers. Let's take a closer look at the Blame Cycle.

Jim made a mistake, and his manager responded by blaming him for it. Jim responded by getting defensive. It's important to remember that when people get blamed for something, they tend to get defensive because their self-esteem is being threatened.

When Jim got defensive, he began to pass the blame (it's contagious). Jim felt he was blamed for something he wasn't totally responsible for, and this led to an undermining of trust in the relationship. Now, because of a lack of trust, Jim becomes more tentative in his behavior, and less willing to take risks or make decisions. The breakdown of trust and the tendency to avert future risk are crucial junctures in the blame cycle. Let's look at it in more detail.

I believe that people most qualified to solve operational problems are the people closest to the operational level. When people become supervisors or managers, they are often chosen for the role based on their technical expertise. So, if someone is an excellent engineer, the only path to upward mobility in most organizations is to become a manager, supervisor or team leader. However, being the person in charge requires more interpersonal skills than technical skills. Now the engineer must worry about keeping metrics, building teams, creating an empowering motivational environment, providing useful information, feedback and vision. Sometimes, however, it's difficult for some people to make that skills transition. After all, up to now, they have been the technical experts, and they define themselves as such. Some new supervisors and managers find it difficult to "let go" and they tend to become "micromanagers." So, let's apply this notion to the scenario about Jim.

We are now at the Risk Avoidance stage of the Blame Cycle. Let's say a new requirement has come up and the manager asks Jim to take care of it. However, the manager also says that he personally has had a good deal of experience with this type of requirement in the past, so the manager lays out the steps he thinks Jim should follow, and hands Jim the recommended steps to follow. The manager thanks him and walks off. Jim takes a look at the steps, saying to himself "This may have been the way he did it in the past, but we have new applications and processes that I don't think he's aware of. Besides, I've worked with this customer a great deal, and this is not the best way to handle this with her. But if that's what he wants, then that's what I'll give him. Nothing more and nothing less. The last time I tried something different, look where it got me. I'm not about to do that again." So, Jim does exactly what he's told to do, even though he doesn't think it will work because he does it every day, and the manager doesn't. Besides, he doesn't want to take the chance of being blamed again if it doesn't work out. From now on, Jim's modus operandi will be "Just tell me what you want, and that's what I'll give you—even if it's not necessarily the best way to do it."

Folks, if that happens, Jim's creativity is lost, and eventually, his productivity. The cycle didn't really start with the mistake, but with the way the manager *responded* to the mistake by focusing on blame. Interestingly, the irony of the Blame Cycle is that it reinforces a lack of risk-taking and creativity. If things don't work out, the employee can simply say "I was just doing what I was told to do. So, don't blame me. The manager told me to do it this way." Consequently, the employee may not feel as empowered and accountable for their actions, become less creative and productive, and the manager continues to lose trust in the employee's abilities. No one wins.

Looking at the Blame Cycle within the context of the "3 Things," much could be avoided or resolved if clear **expectations** were set initially when the manager asked Jim to take on the project. Also, when the mistake was made, if the manager made his or her **intentions** clear that blame was not an option, but focused on accountability and learning from the mistake, and finally, if the manager took time to **acknowledge** the effort and focused on coaching rather than blaming.

Earlier, I said the Blame Cycle occurs every day in organizations and relationships. If that's the case, besides looking at the situation through the lens of the "3 Things," what else can be done about it? First, it's useful to look at mistakes as opportunities for learning (reframing). Mistakes are necessary for better understanding, not things that must be expunged. If mistakes are viewed as opportunities, the following tool can be extremely useful.

A Tool to Avoid Blame and Focus on Learning

A number of years ago, the US Military came up with a tool that can be used both at work and at home. It's called the *After-Action Review* (AAR). The tool consists of four basic questions. The questions are simple, but it takes considerable effort to keep them focused properly. The AAR can be used whenever a mistake, or even a success has occurred. Using the previous example of Jim, the manager might have sat down with Jim and any significant others, and asked the following four questions:

AAR
(After Action Review)

> **What Happend?**
> **(Stay Focused on facts - not people)**

> **Why do you think it happend?**
> **(Stay focused on facts - not people)**

> **What did you / we learn?**
> **(Focus on Learning - not blaming)**

> **What should be done about it going forward?**

It's important to **stay focused on facts rather than people** in order to avoid falling into the trap of the blame game. In the AAR, the focus is also on learning, not blaming. It's action-oriented and future-focused—and it works! I use it in my training, consulting and coaching projects quite often, and it can also be used at home with spouses, children, and grandchildren!

I urge you to use the **AAR** in order to avoid the natural tendency to blame when mistakes and problems occur. Remember, it's all about the way you *respond!*

Chapter 8

Informal, Formal Organizational Communication and Use of Technology

In this chapter, I will focus on the organizational context and how informal and formal communication processes can affect organizational outcomes. Let's look at informal communication first.

Informal Communication (Grapevine)

Think about some of the information you've received via the "grapevine." Things like who's in line for a promotion; organizational changes being considered; who's going to take over a new project, and so on. The reality of organizational life is that much of the information you receive is via the informal channels that operate in every complex organization. These informal channels are often referred to as the "grapevine." If you manage, it would be particularly useful to know the general characteristics of grapevine activity, and to have some methods of coping with it in your own organization. Some of the original grapevine research was conducted by Keith Davis (1967). Let's look at some things known about the grapevine:

1. The grapevine is fast. There are generally few restrictions on the grapevine because it's usually transmitted personally or via instant messaging, texting, and email. Consequently, it doesn't follow any chain of command. It is undoubtedly the fastest way to spread information in an organization.

2. Surprisingly, the research shows that the grapevine is often quite accurate. Research on grapevine activity suggest it to

be seventy-five to ninety-five percent accurate even though the details are incomplete. It's also important to note that the remaining five to twenty-five percent could be critical to the accuracy of the information.

3. Grapevine information, like grapes, usually comes in bunches. It might be assumed that grapevine information travels in a straight line from person A to B to C. Actually, research shows that A might tell three or four others, yet only one or two of them will then pass on the information. These clusters of communication continue until people lose interest or until the issue grows much larger.

4. Grapevine information and rumors are not really the same types of communication, even though they may appear to be. Rumors are usually unfounded, unsubstantiated bits of information, while grapevine information will likely be more factual in nature, based on an event or decision. Rumors can cause real problems for managers. Ideally, rumors should be stopped as soon as possible because they can distort employees' perceptions about decisions and future events.

What can a manager do about grapevine activity and rumors? Well, the first thing to remember is that you can't stop them from occurring. They are as inevitable as rain. A manager can, however, learn ways to control both rumors and grapevine activity:

- Once a rumor has begun, make sure those who are most affected by it are given the most accurate and timely information available.

- Use effective, consistent communication channels to convey accurate, timely information, e.g., internal email, newsletters, video teleconferencing, instant messaging, FaceTime, Zoom, etc.

- Identify your "locally influential" employees (those employees who are well respected and have high credibility among their peers), and make sure they have the accurate, consistent information.

- Research shows that first-line supervisors have significant influence on the people that directly report to them. Make sure the first-line supervisors have accurate, consistent and repeatable messages to be conveyed to the operational level employees.

Grapevine and rumors go into overdrive during times of change. Again, keeping the first-line supervisors well informed with a consistent, accurate, repeatable and supportive message about the change initiative is extremely important for a smoother transition to occur. In my opinion, the first line supervisor is key to effective change management, so it's extremely important that they have the correct information to convey to those most affected by the change.

Recognizing that these same methods are appropriate in our personal lives, isn't providing accurate, consistent, repeatable and supportive messages to our spouses, kids and significant others important as well? When we are talking with our family and friends, can we honestly say that we are consistent, accurate and supportive in our communication? For example, after fifty-eight years of marriage, I've learned that parents must always try to be consistent, accurate (unambiguous) and supportive when communicating with their children. The same applies to single-parent households as well. If we don't see ourselves communicating in this manner, it might be an area worth working on. I find that I often need to work on it because I'm not always consistent and accurate in my communication. I think we all tend to be "works in progress" when it comes to communication.

Formal Communication in Organizations:

While information coming from managers and supervisors may be considered formal communication, we can expand on it by considering the legitimacy, official nature and direction of the information being conveyed. One of the areas of research in organizational communication has focused, is on the direction of the communication. Formal organizational communication messages move in three basic directions: downward, upward, and horizontal. Let's take a closer look at each direction.

Downward Communication refers to those messages that flow vertically from managers to direct reports and individual contributors. There are essentially seven types of downward communication:

1. **Task Instructions: The What** ("Please send this information to the following people.")

2. **Task Rationales: The Why** ("We need to do it this way because it will be less expensive.")

3. **Organizational Policies:** ("Please review our inclement weather policy.")

4. **Position Descriptions:** ("These are the duties of a HR Assistant...")

5. **Performance Feedback:** ("Your report was clear, accurate and timely.")

6. **Mission Statement or Organizational Goals:** ("Our job in Public Affairs is to publicize the Department's programs.")

7. **Technological or Organizational Change Initiatives:** ("On January 10, we are rolling out the new software application.")

Although downward communication in organizations has been extensively studied, significant problems exist regarding "information underload" and "information overload." For example, how do you feel when you need important information and you can't get it? Frustrated? Angry? It's quite frustrating when ambiguity surrounds an important situation, or when you can't move forward with a decision or action until you receive certain information, and you're not getting it. If you are a manager, you have the ongoing challenge of providing people with the information they need, without overburdening them with extra, unnecessary information that they don't need. Maintaining this balance is challenging for any manager, supervisor or team leader.

Another potential issue with downward communication is whether it is timely. Management not only jeopardizes its credibility with untimely information, but it also creates a ripe climate for rumors. In a series of studies across sixteen organizations, Goldhaber and his associates (1977) concluded the following:

- Most employees don't receive the information they need to do their jobs effectively.

- The primary information needs of employees are about personal job-related matters, and secondarily about organizational decision-making.

- The best information sources (accuracy, timeliness, etc.) are the employees' immediate supervisors and coworkers. The worst information source appears to be top management.

- Across the sixteen studies, information from top management appeared to be of lower quality than from other sources within the employees' immediate environment.

Even though immediate supervisors appear to be more effective information sources than higher levels of management, there are still problems that exist. Over the years, when I conducted organizational diagnosis projects, I normally interviewed a cross-section of employees in order to get a representative sample from each organizational level. One of the questions I would ask employees was "How do you know if you are doing a good job?" They would usually say "What do you mean?" I would then say, "What are the indicators that let you know you're doing a good job?" Overwhelmingly, participants would say they weren't always sure, and that "No news is good news." I would often hear participants say that as long as they didn't hear anything from their supervisors, they assumed they were doing okay, because the only feedback they tended to receive was when there was a problem or issue that needed to be resolved. So—no news is good news. With that said, many participants added that they didn't like the situation because they didn't know "where they stood" with their supervisors, and they were unclear about what was **expected** of them. They would often say they that because of the lack of feedback, they didn't feel **acknowledged** for their work, and weren't sure what their supervisor really thought of them. (**Unclear** *Intentions*)

Upward Communication

Upward communication refers to those messages that flow up the organization from direct reports and individual contributors to managers and supervisors. Having a free flow of information up the organizational chain is critically important to overall effectiveness by providing managers and supervisors with the feedback necessary to solve problems and make decisions. Additionally, it allows for more employee involvement in problem-solving and decision-making. Effective upward communication is critical for a number of reasons:

- It helps management understand its downward communication needs better.

- It increases the likelihood that employees will accept decisions because they've had an opportunity to be heard, by participating in the process.

- It provides feedback about how well downward messages are understood and accepted.

- It provides insight into how employees think and feel about their jobs, achievements and challenges, their internal/external customers and their organization.

- It provides management with a better understanding and insight into what's going well and what's not going well.

- It provides management with a better understanding of internal and external customer needs and expectations.

- It provides management with information to help the organization be more proactive in meeting its mission requirements.

If you manage, you want to nurture those formal and informal opportunities to solicit information on how things are going in their operation. Upward communication can be solicited through employee coaching, counseling, mentoring sessions, staff meetings, in-house publications, suggestion systems and online surveys. These are just a few vehicles by which upward communication can be solicited. However, be aware that three things can affect upward communication accuracy: **Trust, Employees' Upward Mobility Aspirations** and **Perceived Upward Influence of the Manager**. With these three variables in play, the information managers receive from their direct reports and individual contributors could be distorted—in the direction of telling managers what they want to hear! Let's take a closer look:

Trust:

The degree by which the manager is trusted could dramatically influence the accuracy of the information going upward. For example, if the direct report doesn't trust the manager, it is likely he or she will be reticent to give candid information. For example, if the direct report doesn't trust the manager, and the manager asks how the project is going, the employee might feel internal pressure to say "Great!" even though that may not be true. If the employee doesn't trust the manager's reaction to problems, it might be easier to avoid talking about them. Consequently, the manager may make decisions based on invalid information.

Upward Mobility Aspirations:

This lack of trust leading to distorted upward communication is magnified if the employee has upward mobility aspirations to move up in the organization. The employee may think his or her promotion or reputation could be negatively affected by presenting a more accurate, but less positive picture of a situation.

Perceived Upward Influence:

If the employee thinks the manager has significant influence in the upper echelons of the organization, doesn't trust the manager, and has upward mobility aspirations, there will be a much greater likelihood of distortion because the potential impact could be greater. It's important to note that if the employee **does** trust the manager, upward mobility aspirations and perceived upward influence are not as significant. The most significant factor appears to be the level of trust in the relationship. More trust leads to more accurate upward communication. Less trust, particularly when upward mobility aspirations and upward influence are part of the mix, leads to less accurate upward communication.

Horizontal Communication

Horizontal communication deals with the lateral flow of information in organizations. This information flow may be across departments, groups, divisions, etc. It may also be information flow within workgroups and among peers in the form of collaboration.

Among the major barriers to horizontal communication are the different values, perceptions, assumptions, language and loyalties held by people in different parts of the organization. For example, in your own experience, how often have you seen problems between line and staff personnel; between research and development and operations; between engineering and accounting; or between human resource specialists and budget analysts? Horizontal communication is necessary for effective task coordination, teamwork, information sharing, problem-solving and decision-making. As organizations grow in size, the jobs become more specialized. While specialization is necessary, the more effective organizations make a conscious effort to coordinate and integrate those specialized functions toward achieving the organization's mission. This coordination is often achieved by the creation of cross-functional teams, and a culture that emphasizes and supports the importance of information sharing across functional components.

One of the helpful ways to approach effective horizontal communication is to think of all of the people we interface with in order to meet certain objectives or meet requirements. When considering them, think of those coworkers and peers as "Process Customers." These Process Customers are those individuals up or down the line who add value in meeting organizational goals and requirements. I will talk more about Process Customers in a later chapter.

Organizational Climate

Much emphasis is often placed on how different generations view work, and we've likely read or heard how younger employees have different values and must be managed differently. I'm not a big fan of emphasizing differences along generational lines. I'm not discounting some of that research, but in my opinion, most employees want a communication climate that fosters achievement, recognition and the opportunity to have an impact. I don't think I'm being overly naïve by thinking that most people want to do a good job, be recognized and feel they have an influence on outcomes—at work and in their personal lives. I think supervisors and managers must be careful not to stereotype people based on their particular generation—and vice versa!

A few years ago, Buckingham & Coffman (1999), two researchers from the Gallup Polling organization, conducted a massive study in which they had in-depth interviews with over 80,000 managers across over 400 organizations. Their findings are significant to our understanding of organizational climate; what a healthy climate looks like and why people want to stay. One of their conclusions is that **people do not leave organizations. They leave managers.**

Based on their research, the authors concluded there are twelve questions that capture the characteristics and essence of an organizational climate, and that effective managers will foster these characteristics. They represent a climate where people can contribute, prosper and want to stay. I've modified the list of twelve questions by providing a space for you to answer **Yes, No**, or **Sometimes**. Your answers may give you some insight into your own work environment, and why you might feel the way you do about it. Let's take a look at the twelve questions.

The 12 Questions

If employees can answer each of the following 12 questions affirmatively, a strong workplace is likely to exist. If you want to try it, indicate **Y=Yes; N=No; S=Sometimes**

1. Do I know what is expected of me at work? _____

2. Do I have the equipment and material I need to do my work right? _____

3. At work, do I have the opportunity to do what I do best every day? _____

4. In the last 7 days, have I received recognition or praise for good work? _____

5. Does my supervisor or someone at work seem to care about me as a person? _____

6. Is there someone at work who encourages my development? _____

7. At work, do my opinions seem to count? _____

8. Does the mission/purpose of my organization make me feel my work is important? _____

9. Are my coworkers committed to doing quality work? _____

10. Do I have a best friend at work? _____

11. In the last six months, have I talked to someone about my progress? _____

12. This last year, have I had opportunities at work to learn and grow? _____

Take a look at your answers. The more **Y**'s you have would indicate that you very likely love your job; feel you are making contributions in a challenging role; feel you are being acknowledged for those contributions, and you will likely remain in the organization.

The more **N**'s you have would indicate that you may not like your job as much; may not feel the job is a good "fit" for you; may not be acknowledged enough for your contributions, and will more likely leave if the opportunity presents itself. The more **S**'s you have might indicate a level of engagement and satisfaction that is not always high, but possibly acceptable to you and your manager.

Rule of Thumb: The more your answers are in the affirmative, the more engaged and satisfied you likely are, with little likelihood that you will leave. The more answers in the negative, the less engaged and satisfied you likely are, with a higher likelihood that you will leave.

If you manage, you may want to try this. Take a look at the twelve questions again. However, this time, change the "I" to "they"; change "me" to "them"; change "my" to "their." Then answer the questions again. This may give you some insight into your own managerial behavior, what you think you're doing well, and what you think you may need to work on.

Lastly, you might also change some of the organizationally pertinent questions, while retaining the essence of the questions. Then ask the twelve questions within the context of your home environment, or in some of your more significant non-work relationships and see how you fare. For example, just to name a few, at home or in our personal relationships, don't we want to know what's expected of us? Don't we want the right tools and information in order to do the jobs that need to be done around the house, and receive recognition from our spouses or significant others when we get those jobs done? Don't we want people in our personal lives to care about us and encourage our development? When we are discussing family issues, or when we are among friends, don't we want our opinions to count? Don't we want everyone in our family to pitch in and do their part in doing the best job they can do? Don't we want to feel cared for, supported, and know that the people that are close to us, care about our development and progress? Don't we appreciate when our spouse, or other important people in our lives, support opportunities to learn and grow? Again, much of what works in the organizational context is the same as what works in our homes and relationships outside of the organization.

One more thing about organizational climate. A few years ago, I conducted surveys and interviews with approximately 1900 employees across five organizations in the Washington, DC, metropolitan area, and found some interesting, corroborating findings. While I won't present all of the findings, here are some interesting things employees said they wanted from their immediate supervisors and managers.

- Easy to Talk To

- Tries to See the Merit in My Ideas

- Helps People Understand Organizational Goals

- Keeps Employees Informed (Highest Correlation with Job Satisfaction)

- Consistent High Expectations Followed by Feedback

- Keeps Promises (Highest Correlation with Satisfaction with Supervisor)

- Has High Ethical Standards

- Focuses on Accountability & Empowerment — Not Blame

So, what might we conclude from the above list?

- If you supervise or manage — or if you are a parent, husband, wife, friend, etc., try to manage your relationships by being friendly, engaging, and easy to talk to. Make it "safe" for the other person.

- Acknowledge others' ideas by seeing the merit in them, instead of discounting or disagreeing with them. It doesn't mean you must agree with everything they say, but it does mean looking for those ideas you can acknowledge as having worth.

- Try to understand and support others to achieve their goals, even if you don't agree with them.

- Keep appropriate people sufficiently informed about things that are important and necessary to them. (Regression analysis showed this was a major predictor of job satisfaction.)

- Be consistent with what you expect from others. When your expectations are met, let people know through your feedback that you appreciate their effort.

- Keep your promises. I know I've said it before, but if you say you are going to do something, then you must do it! The quickest way to lose our credibility with others is to not keep our promises. ((Regression analysis showed this was the major predictor of satisfaction with immediate supervisors.)

- Be ethical in all of your actions. People judge us by our actions, and as I said before, the higher up you go in the organization, everything you do or don't do will be observed and evaluated. It comes with the territory.

- Be accountable for your own actions, and don't be reticent to hold others accountable for theirs. People tend to hold themselves more accountable when they know they are not going to be blamed or chastised for their mistakes. **Focus on learning — not blaming.**

Chapter 9

Meetings, Meeting, Meetings!

While many of our meetings may be held virtually, we still must participate in face-to-face meetings. Some of us may also feel we spend too much time in them. Over the years, I've asked approximately 2,000 federal employees (first and mid-level supervisors) how much time they think they spend in meetings while at work. I defined meetings as formally called sessions, not hallway or unscheduled conversations. The average percentage of time spent by those employees questioned was over fifty percent. More than half of their time was being spent in meetings. I also asked two follow-up questions concerning the meetings they attended. First, I asked how many meetings they considered to be beneficial in getting their jobs done. The answer was that only thirty percent of the meetings were considered beneficial! Second, I asked why they felt the meetings were unproductive. The following reasons were typical:

- "Don't know what the goals of the meeting are."
- "Meetings run longer than the time allotted."
- "Don't know why I was asked to attend."
- "Don't know what material I need in preparation for the meeting."
- "People don't listen to one another."
- "Everyone's got a hidden agenda."
- "Meetings are chaotic. There's no control over procedures."
- "No opportunity to give my opinion. I might as well be sent an email."

- "We have heated arguments which lead us off the topic."

- "Doesn't seem to be much in the meeting's objective."

- "The people who have the most information about the problem often aren't asked to attend the meeting."

- "We just seem to go around in circles."

To those of us who have spent much time in meetings, none of this is news. We have expressed or heard these sentiments before. The purpose of this chapter is to offer some insight and skills for dealing with the problems that can arise when people have a meeting.

First, we'll briefly examine some of the different types of meetings formed in organizations. Secondly, I'll make both general and specific suggestions on how to improve the effectiveness of the various types of meetings. Last, I'll provide a pre-meeting checklist, a checklist for conducting meetings and a checklist for post-meeting activities.

Types of Group Meetings

Every organization, regardless of its size or objective, gets work done by using group meetings, face-to-face, and virtually by video and audio teleconferencing. While there may be many types of meetings, for our purposes, these task-oriented meetings will be classified by type and function:

Types of meetings:

- Status Meetings

- Information Sharing Meetings

- Problem-Solving/Decision-Making Meetings

- Training Meetings

Status Meetings

Status meetings often include updates on projects, goals, challenges, etc. They are usually conducted on a regular basis throughout a project's lifecycle. Their primary goal is to keep relevant members updated on progress, challenges, due dates and future steps. These types of meetings usually use visually oriented tools such as PowerPoint to more effectively convey the informational updates.

Information Sharing Meetings

Information sharing meetings are designed to share information about decisions made, new policies and operational changes, new products, etc. These types of meetings also tend to use visually oriented tools such as PowerPoint to more effectively share the information, making it more meaningful and memorable.

Problem-Solving/Decision-Making Meetings

Problem-solving meetings are much more complex and challenging than other types of meetings. Some of those challenges and complexities pertain to sufficiently sharing the necessary information, keeping people focused, making sure the correct problem and root causes have been identified and defined, working through personal views, hidden agendas, "turf" issues and power struggles, just to name a few variables that can affect outcomes. Additionally, it is necessary to have a structure that's inclusive and focused to move the group forward to a viable decision.

Training Meetings

Keeping the workforce well trained and working effectively are critical objectives of effective organizations. A number of years ago at a conference, the CEO of a major organization was making a presentation describing his organization's efforts to keep its workforce well trained both technically and interpersonally. During the question and answer period, an audience member made the point that if the CEO's organization is putting so much time, energy and resources into training its people, the organization is likely making them more effective, but also more negotiable in the job market. The audience member then asked, "Aren't you afraid they might leave?" The CEO's response was wonderful. He said "Yes, but what if we don't train our people and they stay?" Essentially, organizations must invest in their employees by keeping them technically and interpersonally proficient, with the feeling that they are essential members of their team, department, etc. The necessity of feeling competent and being an integral part of something we admire are vital components of an effective organization.

Some General Questions to Be Answered Regarding Any Type of Meeting

Over the years, at the university and in my training and consulting business, I've had to run all of the four types of meetings described earlier. There is a question I usually ask myself before I even call a meeting, and that's "What do I want to accomplish by the end of this meeting?" If the answer to that question is uncertain, I seriously consider not having the meeting until I am clear about what I want to accomplish. Too often, we have meetings for a reason rather than a purpose. A reason may be "It's Thursday, and we always meet on Thursday." or "We're meeting to hash out some ideas." Neither of these two statements mention what the meeting leader intends to accomplish by the end of the meeting. Consequently, the goal isn't clear and that usually leads to an ineffective meeting. The answer to the question "What do I want to accomplish by the end of this meeting?" becomes the stated purpose of the meeting. The meeting's purpose might be stated as "By the end of the meeting we will..." or "The purpose of this meeting is to...." Whatever the meeting goal is, it should be behavioral and future-oriented. When people know what the meeting's purpose is, they have more clarity about why the meeting is being held and why they are attending.

This takes us to the second question I ask before the meeting. "Who must attend in order for us to accomplish the meeting's goal?" Having the right people in the room or on the video/audio teleconference is essential to having a productive meeting. If attendees are asking themselves why they have been asked to attend, then they may not have a clear understanding of how they can contribute or what's expected of them.

The third question to ask is "What do I and the attendees need to do in order to prepare for this meeting?" It's such a waste of resources and everyone's time if the meeting leader and or the attendees have not fully prepared for the meeting by not having the necessary information or expertise. If a cost/benefit analysis were run on meetings, the results could be staggering. Obviously, every meeting is different, but if you take into consideration salaries, energy and facilities, travel, etc., then the cost could be significant. Let's take an average weekly meeting of five managers on a management team. Let's say the average annual salary is $100,000 per person, and they spend an average of fifteen hours per week in these team meetings. In this scenario, the weekly meeting cost for only these five people is $4,076, and the annual cost is $212,000! The online scheduling service Doodle released the results of a 2019 study of nineteen million meetings and interviews with more than 6,500 working professionals in the US, UK and Germany. In the US alone, the cost of meetings was estimated to be $399 billion! According to the report, respondents most often cited the following problems:

- I don't have enough time to do the rest of my work (44 percent) **(Expectations violated, lack of acknowledgment of attendees' time)**

- Unclear actions lead to confusion (43 percent) **(Unclear expectations and intent)**

- Bad meeting organization results in a loss of focus on projects (38 percent) **(Expectations violated)**

- Irrelevant attendees slow progress (31 percent) **(Expectations violated)**

No matter what type of meeting is held, the meeting leader and attendees can benefit by paying attention to the following seven things:

- Setting clear objectives for the meeting beforehand

- Informing invitees why their attendance is necessary, and what information they need to have for the meeting

- Having a clear agenda, and distributing ahead of time if possible

- Having the right people in the meeting

- Having the right number of people in the room (this could change if the meeting is virtual)

- Set ground rules for the meeting. (This helps add focus and structure)

- Using visual stimuli such as PowerPoint, flip charts, white board, etc.

I remember talking to a senior manager about the cost/benefits of meetings, and thought his response was memorable. He jokingly said "That does it. I'm going to call a meeting to cancel all further meetings!"

At this point, let's take a look at the communication tools, roles and responsibilities for meeting leaders and attendees for each of the four types of meetings:

Status Meetings:

Leader's Communication Tools:

- Setting expectations on procedure by establishing ground rules, priorities, time frames and process

- Active Listening (paraphrasing, reflecting, asking closed, open, clarifying questions

- Acknowledging contributions

- Using SBIS and the AAR when appropriate

Attendees' Communication Tools:

- Active Listening (paraphrasing, reflecting, asking closed, open, clarifying questions

- Acknowledging contributions

- Using SBIS and the AAR when appropriate

Information Sharing Meetings:

Leader's Communication Tools:

- Setting expectations on procedure by establishing ground rules, priorities, time frames and process

- Active Listening (paraphrasing, reflecting, asking closed, open, clarifying questions

- Acknowledging contributions

- Using SBIS and the AAR when appropriate

Attendees' Communication Tools:

- Active Listening (paraphrasing, reflecting, asking closed, open, clarifying questions

- Acknowledging contributions

- Using SBIS and the AAR when appropriate

Problem-Solving/Decision-Making Meetings:

Leader's Communication Tools:

- Setting expectations on procedure by establishing ground rules, priorities, time frames and process

- Active Listening (paraphrasing, reflecting, asking closed, open, clarifying questions

- Acknowledging contributions

- Using SBIS and the AAR when appropriate

Attendees' Communication Tools:

- Active Listening (paraphrasing, reflecting, asking closed, open, clarifying questions

- Acknowledging contributions

- Using SBIS and the AAR when appropriate

Training Meetings: (Leader's role is more of a Facilitator)

Leader's Communication Tools:

- Setting expectations on procedure by establishing ground rules, priorities, time frames and process

- Facilitates discussion

- Focus on experiential learning (Learning by doing, followed by feedback)

- Active Listening (paraphrasing, reflecting, asking closed, open, clarifying questions

- Acknowledging contributions

- Using SBIS and the AAR when appropriate

Attendees' Communication Tools:

- Active Listening (paraphrasing, reflecting, asking closed, open, clarifying questions

- Participation in experiential activities such as role-playing, case studies, discussion, brainstorming and practice in the learning of new skills and approaches

- Acknowledging contributions

- Using SBIS and the AAR when appropriate

Repeating the leader and attendee skills for each of the first three meeting types is an effort to make a point. Even though the various meetings may have different objectives, the communication skills required are similar for both leader and attendee. They are generic. Although the meeting goals may be different, we can use those same skills to actively participate and contribute to an effective meeting. However, the skills required in a Training meeting are somewhat different. Let's take a closer look.

The leadership model to be used in training meetings should be as experiential as possible. In considering my own leadership style in training meetings, I see my role as that of a facilitator. I use *short* mini-lecture/discussions while paying attention and inviting discussion, based on the experiences and skills people bring with them to the sessions.

The short mini-lecture/discussion is often followed by video modeling of the behaviors that I want the participants to learn. After discussing the video modeling of the behaviors, I will usually have the attendees practice the behaviors in the form of role-plays, using real organizational issues that attendees might experience on the job. I often use the **ATSD** Model. The model looks like this:

Ask: Asking the participants open, closed and clarifying questions about some work-related topic or issue. The participants brainstorm and discuss communication strategies and ways to handle the issue.

Tell: I usually add my own views on the subject being discussed by either acknowledging the participants' contribution or adding my own additional views.

Show: Whenever possible, I will follow up on this discussion with a short video that models the behaviors that we've been discussing.

Do: After the group has had the opportunity to explore, develop and see the skills through video modeling, I have them practice the skills. This practice usually occurs in the form of role-plays. I almost always prefer the role-plays to address real issues rather than my creating hypothetical scenarios to be role-played. While this is my preference, relevant hypothetical role play scenarios can be useful as well. I also organize the role-play activities in such a way that peer-to-peer feedback and discussion can take place after each role-play scenario.

A quick comment about role-playing in training meetings. I think role-playing, followed by participant feedback is one of the most effective techniques for learning new behavioral skills. It is often confused with "acting." Some may disagree, but I don't think role-playing is acting. While the participants start out in a particular role, they should respond to what is actually being said to them. If what is said, makes them feel defensive, then they should respond defensively. However, if a participant uses the skills effectively, the other person should respond accordingly. In other words, the participants respond to what is actually being said to them. They are not "acting." If the role-plays are followed up by participant feedback on what went well and what could have been done differently, a great deal of learning can take place. I believe the true nature of adult learning is that adults learn from other adults, and role-playing is an effective way for adults to learn from one another.

Role-playing is not limited to the work environment. It can also be used as a learning tool at home and in our interpersonal lives as well. Please let me give some personal examples: When I have a meeting coming up, and want some useful feedback on how to approach it, I will often role-play the meeting scenario with my wife, and she will offer very useful feedback on how she thought it went.

Additionally, when my wife has an up-coming meeting she might be concerned about, we will role-play her meeting, and I will provide feedback to her. This allows both of us to practice our approach in a safe environment, and it is always helpful.

One more example if you don't mind. As I've mentioned before, my wife and I have been blessed with three sons (and seven grandchildren). My wife and I have always thought it was important for our boys to have a healthy appreciation for work. Consequently, they had part-time jobs while they were still quite young. We also encouraged them to play sports (soccer and swimming) as well, because we felt that sports were equally important in their development. Our kids didn't always agree with their bosses, their coaches and sometimes their teachers. When they would bring these issues up at the dinner table or living room, my wife and I would ask them questions to get a better understanding of the situation. Once we felt we understood the circumstances, we would often say "Okay, why don't I take on the role of your (coach, boss or teacher). If you wanted to talk with me about your concerns, what would you say to me? How would you go about it?" We would then role-play the discussion, and my wife and I would provide feedback on how it went. We would also recommend alternative approaches if necessary. If the person our kids were concerned about was a man, I would role-play it. If the person was a woman, my wife would role-play it, but it wasn't always necessary to be that precise, because it was the skills we were practicing, regardless of gender. I hope you don't mind that I continue being a corny but proud father for a moment. If you do mind, that's unfortunate, because I'm going to be one anyway. We are very proud of our sons' career and personal successes. Our oldest son is Senior Manager of National Security at one of the largest companies in America. Our middle son is an IT manager at the National Archives, and our youngest son is Chief Human Resources Officer at a large Fortune 100 pharmaceutical company. I will certainly not be so presumptuous as to suggest they are in their positions because when they were younger, we role-played situations and provided feedback to them. Although, they have all said that my wife and I were helpful in teaching them skills that have benefited them in their relationships and their careers. However, let me be clear. What our sons have accomplished is because of their intellects, tenacity, and hard work. Nevertheless, it was sure nice to hear them acknowledge my wife's and my effort to help along the way.

Use of Technology

The use of instant messaging (IM), text messaging, email, video teleconferencing (VTC), and the use of technologies such as Zoom, Skype, Webex, Google Meet, and Microsoft Teams, just to name a few, have become important meeting tools for virtual communication in organizations and our personal lives. We use these technologies to ask questions, convey information, collaborate with others on projects, and keep in contact with friends and colleagues. Email, IM, and texting have changed the very essence of the way we communicate with others both on and off the job. They allow us to share information more easily in a very efficient manner. We can maintain contact with remote colleagues, family members, and friends in a less intrusive way. Especially during the COVID-19 debacle, these technologies have become an integral necessity in doing our work, meeting with key people and team members and maintaining our personal relationships. I've also become more accustomed to conducting training classes via the use of Zoom.

While these technologies have made life so much easier, they are not without potential problems. For example, IM can pose potential security risks, and the "always on, always available" culture can lead to intrusiveness and potential burnout. In my opinion, one of the major issues with virtual technologies is that their overuse leads to less face-to-face communication. This could lead to less effective interpersonal skills both inside and outside of work. Whether using email, IM, texting, or video conferencing software, it's a good idea to establish agreed upon expectations or "ground rules" for their use. Let's take a look at IM first.

Here's a list of things to consider regarding the use of IM or textng. These recommendations could apply to email as well.

- Keep your message short. Keeping your messages short and focused, especially when chatting with a group, will limit any confusion.

- Establish a "charter" regarding the use of IM/texting. This charter may be focused on the technical use of IM/texting as well as the appropriate interpersonal parameters of our chats, such as being respectful, no cursing, keeping our messages focused and short, etc.

- Apply a status-criteria, such as "busy," "away from my desk," or "do not disturb" messages when the person is busy and doesn't want to be interrupted. Additionally, always check and respect the other person's status before sending a message.

- Asking for permission to chat is always a good idea before going further, since we have no idea what the other person is doing at the time.

- It's important to respectfully say "no" when you are busy. Of course, remember to say that you will contact them later.

- Adapt your communication style and choice of words to the receiver of your message. Keeping your message short, focused and professional should generally be the rule.

- Avoid chatting about confidential information such as security issues, corporate strategy or personal information about others.

- Limit your use of IM/texting to deliver personal or negative feedback. These types of messages are best provided face-to-face.

- Be sure to check any documents sent via IM for viruses before sending.

- Try to limit the use of IM/texting for things that are urgent. Email may be a better means of communicating information that lacks urgency.

- Don't confuse work and personal IM/texting accounts.

When using IM, texting, or email, please remember the following five C's. They're good reminders:

1. Concise

2. Clear

3. Correct

4. Complete

5. Courteous

Videoconferencing Tools

Teleworking has been on the upswing for a number of years. Long before COVID-19, organizations have been recognizing the value of working virtually. Videoconferencing has allowed workers to continue having meetings from anywhere from across the globe, across the country, or from one's kitchen or living room. It also satisfies the social interaction many workers often crave when they are working from home. When we videoconference from home, we are letting people we may not normally invite into our living room, and this can feel strange for some. Here are some Do's and Don'ts for videoconferencing that you might find useful.

"Ground rules" for Videoconferencing

- **Be punctual**: Be sure to arrive on time for the videoconference. Be sure to end on time.

- **Be engaging**: Introduce yourself. Be sure others have also introduced themselves. If someone arrives late, have them introduce themselves.

- **Be courteous:** Jot down the names of the other attendees so you can acknowledge their contributions and address them by name. Make sure your phone is turned off or the ringer is turned down to minimize disruptions. Treat the video conference the same you would in an onsite meeting.

- **Pay attention to the lighting:** Adjust the lighting so that you have good light shining at you from the front. You will come across much better over the video.

- **Follow the same guidelines as you do at onsite meetings:** Minimize any distracting mannerisms such as clicking your pen, tapping your fingers, yawning, eating or chewing gum.

- **Please don't multitask:** Remember that people can see you. Show attentiveness when others are speaking and be sure to maintain eye contact with the camera.

- **Please dress appropriately:** Use your best judgment here. You probably know what's appropriate.

- **Conduct video calls from your desk or other appropriate location**. Sitting in your bathrobe at the kitchen table or lying on the couch with your laptop on your chest is generally not a flattering picture.

- **Check your software before the videoconference:** Be sure to test your audio and video before a scheduled call.

- **Keep your space as private as possible: no high traffic areas**. If you have a spouse or small children, try to position yourself in an area that will be relatively private, without a lot of "traffic."

- **Close unused applications**: Utilizing video can be very CPU/memory intensive.

- **Mute yourself when not speaking:** It can become very distracting if you don't.

- **Organize appropriately:** For longer meetings, try to organize information in ten to fifteen-minute segments. This helps to keep everyone more engaged.

- **Time zones:** Be considerate of other participants' time zones. If possible, try to schedule the meeting within participants' workday.

- **Login information:** A few days before the videoconference, send out login information and details to everyone involved. This information can include instructions for logging in, the agenda, list of attendees and meeting start/finish times.

- **Technical support:** It's often useful to assign someone to handle any technology issues that may arise during the meeting. This allows you to focus on keeping the meeting on track.

- **Keep everyone involved:** One of the more significant challenges with virtual meetings is that it's more difficult to get involved and contribute. It is important to pause regularly and ask for attendee input. One way to do this is by using a "round robin" method by asking everyone to comment on a particular subject or issue. Also, using activities or questions that require participation. When people are engaged, it is less likely that they will be distracted. Some meeting platforms allow for participants to virtually "vote" or "raise their hands" in agreement or disagreement on various topics.

Meeting Checklists

The following checklists can be used to help you prepare for, conduct, follow up and evaluate meetings in your organization and elsewhere.

Pre-Meeting Activities Checklist

- What is the purpose of the meeting?

- What are the things to be achieved from the meeting?

- What procedure should I use as the meeting leader?

- Who should be there? How do I view their involvement and impact on the outcome?

- Where should the meeting be held? How long should it last?

- When should it be held?

- What should the participants be told before the meeting?

- Should they prepare anything?

- Should they be sent any material in advance?

- What physical details need to be attended to: room, audio-visual equipment, refreshments?

- What action should be taken after the meeting is over? Will proceedings and results be recorded and disseminated?

Conducting the Meeting Checklist

- Did I make an opening statement that included the purpose, procedures, and ground rules for the meeting?

- Was I patient with differences of opinion?

- Did I actively listen by paraphrasing content, reflecting feelings, and asking closed, open, and clarifying questions?

- Was I aware of my own nonverbal behavior as well as that of other members?

- Did I keep the meeting on track by maintaining appropriate control?

- When I sought information from someone, did I acknowledge the person before asking open or clarifying questions?

Post-Meeting Activities Checklist

- Was the meeting objective(s) achieved?

- What things are to be done now?

  o Actions?
  o Who?
  o Target Date?
- Is there a need for a follow-up meeting?

- Should different meeting procedures be considered for future meetings?

- Were the appropriate people there? Should there be others present if a follow-up meeting is necessary?

- Were the physical facilities sufficient?

- What three things can be done to improve the next meeting?

Meeting Report Forms

Every meeting you lead should be important. Otherwise, it probably wasn't necessary to hold it in the first place. To maximize your communication effectiveness regarding meetings, you may want to send all participants and pertinent nonparticipants a meeting report covering the following areas:

- Organization or unit

- Date and place:

- Called by:

- Attendees:

- Purpose of meeting:

- Topics discussed: (agenda attached if necessary)

- Actions, recommendations, responsibilities, deadlines:

- General comment

Procedures for the Problem-Solving/Decision-Making Meeting

The procedure used to attack problems is usually the leader's responsibility. It is up to the leader to decide on the procedural format or process by which the problem is to be solved. Additionally, the leader must be a catalyst that helps others provide the content or information within those procedures. The following procedural formats might prove helpful to you for your next problem-solving/decision-making meeting:

"Standard" Procedure

What are the limits and nature of the problem(s)?

What are the causes and consequences of the problem(s)?

What characteristics must an acceptable solution have?

What are our alternatives?

Which alternative is the best?

How do we evaluate our solution?

Ideal Solution Form

- Are we all agreed on the nature of the problem?

- What would be the ideal solution from the point of view of all parties involved in the problem?

- What conditions can be changed so that ideal solutions might be achieved?

- Of the solutions available to us, which one approximates the ideal solution?

PERT (Programmed Evaluation Review Technique)

- What is the final event?

- When must it happen?

- What must be accomplished in order to get that final event?

- Diagram a sequential critical path of steps and activities to be done, with time estimates.

- Develop alternatives and contingency routes along the critical pat

Brainstorming

While I described Brainstorming in Chapter 4, I wanted to mention it again in describing an alternate method to weighted voting. The initial process is the same, but the way the information generated is voted upon is different. The meeting leader explains the purpose of the meeting and its procedures, defines the problem, assigns a recorder, and asks the participants to adhere to the following rules:

- Criticism is ruled out.

- Evaluation of ideas must be withheld until later.

- The wilder the ideas, the better. Even offbeat, impractical ideas may trigger ideas in others.

- All ideas are listed on a flip chart. Duplications are removed.

- Quantity is wanted. The greater the number of ideas, the more likelihood of good ones. However, if a participant sees a way to improve on a previous idea, he or she can tell the group so it should be recorded at once.

- After all ideas are listed on the flip chart, each item can be evaluated against a criteria established by the group. The criteria might be Cost, Effect on the Problem, Practicality, Time to Implement, and Management Acceptance. Using a 1-5 scale, each person can vote on the viability of each of the criteria, and the ideas that have the highest scores are then considered more seriously until the group decides on the most appropriate course of action.

- A scribe tallies the votes, and discards or places off to the side items with the lowest scores.

- Another iteration may take place in which there is a final vote for the item(s) chosen.

Brainstorming can be an extremely effective way of generating a large number of ideas in a very short period of time. After all ideas have been recorded, the group can begin prioritizing the ideas and do further analysis. If the communication skills and techniques covered in this chapter are used while conducting meetings, you should become a more effective meeting leader.

Before ending this chapter, I want to remind you of what I've been emphasizing throughout the book. The skills that can work for you in organizational meetings are the same skills that can work for you at home and in your communities. For example, if you and your family were sitting around the kitchen table, trying to decide on where to go on vacation, or whether to buy that new house or car, or which college your son or daughter may want to attend, don't many of these same skills apply? If you are at a homeowners' association meeting or school board meeting, don't many of these same skills apply? Being clear about our expectations, seeking out others' expectations, acknowledging others' contributions, and making our intentions clear and consistent with our behavior, while actively listening and seeking solutions are necessary skills, no matter the context.

Chapter 10

"You Need to Give a Briefing Tomorrow": A Guide to Effective Briefings

In previous chapters, I attempted to show how the skills discussed can apply to our home and interpersonal lives as well. This chapter essentially focuses on delivering briefings or oral presentations in the organizational environment. However, if you must give briefings or presentations in your community, or social clubs, church, etc., you may find this information quite useful. Because most of the work I've done over the years has been with government agencies, I will use the term "briefings" instead of oral presentations, since that is what government agencies call them, and that's what I'm used to saying as well. So, whenever I refer to briefings, I'm referring to oral presentations as well.

A number of years ago, I was asked to develop and deliver a series of two-day courses in "Briefing Technical Material" for a large government agency. The participants were very technical people, and also extremely bright. They were considered "high performers" in the organization, and I thoroughly enjoyed working with them. The internal point of contact was an SIS (Senior Intelligence Service) officer, whom I particularly enjoyed working with. One of his functions was to introduce the course to the attendees. He was highly regarded throughout the agency and his support added a great deal of credibility to this training initiative. During his introduction, he would talk a bit about his extensive career, and talked about a time he was offered an unusual opportunity to advance his career dramatically. However, he was still quite young, and deep down he thought it would be premature to accept the opportunity. The new role would place him in front of the senior leadership in the agency, including the White House. The new role required him to conduct numerous briefings to some extremely high-level people, and it was a risk. He figured this visible role would make him or break him. He decided to accept the new job and was very successful. He also said the reason for his success was his ability to brief upward in the organization, and he would often say of all the "soft" skills that will impact one's career, it was the ability to present effective briefings that benefited him the most. They got him noticed, which in the long run was very career enhancing.

Think about it. Every time you are briefing someone, you are putting your credibility on the line. As I said in an earlier chapter, it takes a long time to develop credibility with others and may take a very short time to lose it. A well-developed, well-delivered 10-minute briefing is one of the quickest ways to enhance your career and upward mobility. However, it's amazing how many people struggle with giving an effective briefing. There are a number of reasons for this. Of course, nervousness is often mentioned when people are asked about giving briefings or presentations of any type. Sometimes, in a training class, I will ask participants at what level of communication do they feel the most comfortable. I break the levels down into one-on-one (interpersonal); small group (sitting around a conference table); or public (briefing or delivering a presentation to an audience). Unsurprisingly, participants say they are more comfortable in interpersonal or small group settings much more than in public settings. Why is that? Obviously people feel more pressure in a public setting because all eyes are on them. In the public context, we are up there "on display" and feeling judged on our performance. In essence, we assume that we can't just "be ourselves" in a public context. We must be more organized, and we must "perform" for the audience. These feelings and assumptions can be nerve-wracking for some of us.

In my opinion, the very act of differentiating between the three levels of communication makes us think we must be something other than ourselves, and that's where the problem is. The people who are most comfortable and ultimately the most effective in a public context such as briefings, are people who don't try to be something other than themselves. Of course, they try to be more structured in the way they present their information, but the more effective briefers are simply "interpersonal" in a public environment. I believe the more interpersonal people are when giving a briefing, the more effective they tend to be. It's best not to try being something you are not. Just be yourself! That's when people tend to be the most comfortable. As I said earlier, you must be structured in presenting the content, but be yourself when you're doing it. Just talk to your audience in your natural manner. It will always be better and more comfortable for you if you do.

Now let's take a closer look at some other issues with briefings. When I was developing the training course in "Briefing Technical Material," I wanted to determine what some of the specific training needs were before developing my training material. Part of my needs analysis consisted of interviews with approximately forty SIS officers. I asked them what problems or concerns they had with the briefings conducted in their organization. I asked them to be specific regarding briefings that were given throughout the agency, at all levels, and they were very willing to talk to me about it.

Below is a list of the major concerns expressed by these senior managers.

- Unclear purpose
- Not doing an audience analysis
- Can't explain visuals or overusing visuals
- Using technical terms/jargon
- Unenthusiastic delivery
- Lack of eye contact
- Inappropriate, distracting gestures/movement

- Disorganized presentation

I'd like to take each of these concerns and give some suggestions on how to deal with them. Let's take a look at the first one.

Unclear Purpose

Several years ago, at a specific Command in the US Navy, there was an important briefing scheduled, and a commander was assigned to present it to a Congressional committee. In preparation, the commander presented a dry run of the briefing to the admiral. After a few minutes into the briefing, the admiral interrupted him, and said he had no idea what the purpose of the briefing was, and as soon as the commander was able to make his purpose clear, he would listen to it again; the admiral then told the commander to leave the room. Unsurprisingly, the commander was devastated, and the situation could also cause serious damage to his career. However, what was unfortunate for him turned out to be very fortunate for me. After the incident with the admiral, I was asked to help the commander develop some of his briefing skills. I worked with him for a couple days. We worked on his organization and his delivery. I also videotaped his briefing, and together we talked about what went well and what could be improved. Thankfully, the commander presented the brief again to the admiral and his staff, and it was accepted by everyone. Let me be clear. The commander had all the necessary intellect and capability to present an excellent briefing. It was simply a matter of structure and a matter of tweaking a few things with his delivery. It became a win-win situation in many ways. The commander conducted himself extremely well with the Congressional committee, and I ended with a contract to conduct more training and employee development activities with the Command.

The reason for the previous example is to emphasize the importance of making your purpose abundantly clear early in the briefing. Don't be reticent to say "The purpose of this briefing is...."

In my opinion, you should state your purpose within the first thirty to sixty seconds of your briefing. When you're not sure of your purpose, or how to articulate it, follow the same suggestion that was recommended for deciding a meeting's purpose. Ask yourself, "What do I want to accomplish by the end of this briefing?" Another way of saying it is, "What do I want the audience to know or do by the end of this briefing?" The answer to those questions becomes your stated purpose. A clear statement of the briefing's purpose sets the **expectation** of what the audience will get from the briefing, so make sure it's clearly stated.

Not Doing an Audience Analysis

Over the years, when I've been asked to conduct a training session or give a presentation, I try to take some time up-front, to ask questions about the people I'm going to be talking to. I try to get answers to some of the following questions: "What will be the organizational level of the audience/participants?" "What level of experience and technical understanding of the topic will the audience/participants have?" "How large will the audience be?" "What audio-visual support will there be?" "Are there any political or organizational realities I need to know about?" "What do they already know?" You may not get complete answers to some of these questions, but they do give you a better understanding of your audience, and what you need to do in order to properly prepare for the briefing or presentation.

Can't Explain Visuals or Overusing Visuals

At work, have you ever given a briefing that was prepared by someone else? If you have, then you probably know how uncomfortable it can be. If it's not your ideas, words and materials such as PowerPoint slides, you may tend to feel disconnected from the information, and it will likely show. It can be especially apparent when you are trying to explain or elaborate on some overly detailed slides. I think it's always best for briefers to create their own slides. If they do, they will feel more in control of the information being presented.

A significant problem with developing PowerPoint slides is the tendency to rely too heavily on them or putting far too much information on them. It's likely that we've seen slides with complete sentences and entire paragraphs. When this happens, it is also likely for the briefer to read directly from the slide, since we are used to reading complete sentences. Additionally, the audience members are probably not paying attention to the briefer because they're reading the slide as well. In which case, why doesn't the briefer just send the slides to the audience and forget about it? When people see complete sentences, they tend to read them. So please, don't use complete sentences on your slides. Use short bullets and short phrases without too many conjunctions, prepositions, adverbs and adjectives in your bullets whenever possible. Keep your bullets simple, while **you** verbally fill in the blanks as you speak to your audience. The slides should complement you, but not replace you.

In order to keep your slides from being too "busy," there's a rule of thumb that can be helpful. Try to use the "6x6 Rule." In other words, try to keep your slides lean. No more than six words across, and six lines down, using short phrases that convey the essence of your message, without using complete sentences. If you are speaking to a larger audience, and you need to use larger text, then maybe a 5x5 rule might work better.

If you intend to spend a fair amount of time on each bullet, you may want to use what can be called "progressive disclosure." In PowerPoint's "Animation" menu, you can select the option of showing one bullet at a time. This keeps the audience where **you** want them to be. If you show all of your bullets at once, the audience will tend to read ahead of you, and you're going to lose a portion of their attention.

How many slides should you use in say, a ten-minute briefing? A simple, yet elegant way of organizing just about anything is Introduction, Body and Conclusion, so I'll use that structure to suggest a formula for determining the number of slides you'll need for a briefing lasting ten-minutes. First of all, you should always have a Title Slide (first slide). This is where you state your briefing's Title and Purpose.

You should then have an Overview or Agenda slide listing the main points you intend to cover (second slide). The Overview slide is important because it tells where you are going to go in the briefing. In other words, it sets the **expectations** for the audience. Think of the Statement of Purpose as your destination, and the Overview of your main points as the route you intend to take in order to get to your destination.

Essentially, but not always, you should have one slide per main point. So, if you have three main points with sub-bullets for support, and one main point per slide, you should now have your third, fourth, and fifth slides.

That takes us to the Conclusion. Always have a Summary slide in your Conclusion (sixth slide). The Summary essentially summarizes the main points and reinforces your Purpose. You don't want to include new information here. You simply want to create a memorable summary of your primary message. Finally, you should have a Question & Answer Slide inviting audience members to ask questions regarding the briefing. This slide may also have some of your contact information on it as well (seventh slide).

Obviously, not every situation is going to be the same, but as a rule of thumb, a ten-minute briefing should have no more than seven slides, using simple phrases as bullets, not using complete sentences if possible, and showing one bullet at a time to keep the audience where you want them to be instead of reading ahead of you.

The effective use of PowerPoint slides can support and enhance your briefing message. However, they must be used carefully so that they don't overcome the briefer. As I said earlier, the slides should complement the briefer, not take the place of the briefer.

Using Technical Terms/Jargon

Another reality of organizational life is that we live in our organizational cultures for eight to ten hours a day, and we speak the language of that culture. We use certain technical terms, acronyms, and other phrases that may be unique to that culture. Consequently, when we deliver a briefing, it's very possible that we may use those same terms that we use every day to an audience that may not be as familiar. It's usually best not to assume your audience will understand all of the terminology you use, unless you are crystal clear about who your audience is. If you are unsure, it's best to define your acronyms, and go a bit overboard in explaining technical terms. For example, if you are speaking to your peers who have a solid grasp of the technical information, it may not be necessary to explain the acronyms or technical terms being used. However, after doing an audience analysis, you know that some audience members will not have a solid grasp of the technical information, it's best to be more careful and explanatory with your terms. Additionally, if you are briefing up the chain, to a group of upper-level managers, they may not want you to get "in the weeds" with your technical information. In those situations, it's best to keep your information at a higher level, without getting too much into the details.

Unenthusiastic Delivery

In an earlier chapter, we had a discussion of the importance of paralanguage. Our voices offer an orchestra of tones, inflections, intensity and pauses. These variations convey how we feel about things, and they add dimension and shading to our words, just as color adds depth and mood to a painting.

In my training and consulting business, I must drive approximately forty miles each way from Maryland to Northern Virginia where my government clients are. During the drives, I try to keep up with the latest research in management, leadership, and communication by listening to audiobooks. I find it to be an effective use of my time while on the road. I remember getting an audiobook that dealt with the research on the role of "interpersonal influence" on relationships. I listened to the first chapter, and then turned it off. The content was fine, but the reader's voice was spoken in a monotone, and the pitch was incredibly irritating to me. The audiobook on the subject of influence, had sufficient content, and actually influenced me a great deal. It influenced me to turn it off! Keep this example in mind when you are giving a briefing. You want to connect with your audience. Your content might be excellent, but if your inflection, pauses, enthusiasm, tone, and intensity are nonexistent or inconsistent with your message, it will be very difficult for people to feel that connection. Essentially, your paralanguage can enhance your content, or it can undermine it.

As I said in an earlier chapter, there's a truism about the world that has been helpful for me to remember. If you take any positive characteristic and carry it to the extreme, it will become a negative. For example, I assume we consider assertiveness to be a good thing. It means standing up for your views and opinions without infringing on the views and opinions of others. If we take assertiveness to one extreme, we may become aggressive when we try to force our views and opinions on others. If we go to the other extreme, we may be overly passive, subordinating our own views and opinions and be taken advantage of. This same notion can be applied to our paralanguage. Speaking in a monotone tells the audience that you are not connecting with anything other than the content you prepared before even meeting them. On the other extreme, a voice that is piercing, with shrill enthusiasm that appears contrived, can be equally ineffective. Either extreme can be problematic. Make a conscious effort in your paralanguage to convey relaxed tones. Punctuate those tones with small bursts of energy to make a point or lift the enthusiasm. Periodically pause for emphasis. The pause can be a very powerful rhetorical tool. Pauses can be used to accentuate a point, or they can be used as an invitation for audience questions and discussion. However, be careful not to use "vocalized pauses" such as "you know" "ahh" or "uhm." The way to help minimize these vocalized pauses, is to remain silent until you are ready to speak. For some reason, people feel they need to continue speaking, so they use these vocalized pauses as fillers. They can be irritating to an audience, and make the speaker look unprepared. In these cases, "Silence is Golden." A pause can actually be a dramatic rhetorical strategy to emphasize the importance of something in your message.

Developing your Paralanguage

One of the best ways I've found to develop effective paralanguage skills is to select a well- known speech or book chapter. Read it out loud. First, read the passage quickly and without pauses. Then, read it again with inflections, emphasis, and appropriate pauses. The difference will be striking, and it will help you feel more comfortable with vocal inflections and pauses when you make your own briefing or presentation.

Lack of Eye Contact

In my business, I've been privileged to speak to hundreds of people a week and thousands over the year. I love to do it, and I feel blessed that I'm still able to do what I love. However, it wasn't always that way. During my first year in college, I took a "Speech" class. I remember having a very difficult time getting up in front of the class and presenting a short, five-minute speech. I was worried about making mistakes, forgetting my words, being laughed at, and I sometimes looked down at my notes more than at my audience. The instructor noticed that I wasn't maintaining very good eye contact, so decided to give me some advice. He told me to pick a few things in the back of the room, just above the heads of the audience members. He then told me to scan those things, and it would appear that I was looking at my audience, but I was not actually looking at them. He said this would help me improve my eye contact. Before I go further, I want to say that is the **worst** piece of advice regarding improving eye contact with your audience. You *need* to look at your audience! I guarantee that if you are scanning objects above your audience's heads, they will know it, and you will lose your connection with them.

Earlier in this chapter, I said the more interpersonal you are with your audience, the more effective you will be. You will not appear interpersonal if you don't maintain eye contact with them. Think of it this way. When you maintain eye contact with your audience, you are "visiting" with them. You can look at individuals or clusters of individuals to visit with for about two to three seconds. Be careful, however, as I mentioned in another chapter, not to look only at certain audience members who give you positive feedback. Try to include all of your audience as much as possible.

Inappropriate, Distracting Gestures/Movement

Appropriate use of gestures and movement can have a significant impact on the briefing's effectiveness. Earlier, I mentioned a training project I was involved in. It consisted of my training a few hundred top performers in the area of "briefing technical material." The participants were part of a select group of "fast trackers" who had strong technical backgrounds. They were very smart but often had difficulty conveying their technical knowledge in a briefing environment. The method I used in the classes was to provide instruction in the form of mini-lectures, discussion and video modeling. I would then assign each participant the responsibility of developing a ten-minute briefing in their area of technical expertise. I would videotape each briefing, and the other participants and I would provide feedback to the briefer. I would follow up by providing one-on-one video feedback in a "breakout" room. There was one briefer in particular who I remember very well. He was extremely bright. The content and organization of his briefing were excellent. However, he would look at the camera with a "deer in the headlights" look. His body was absolutely rigid, with his arms clasped to his side and virtually no body movement in the form of gestures. He was so rigid, that his knees would often "buckle." Actually, they "buckled" quite a bit during his briefing. When we had the one-on-one video session, I played his tape in fast forward, which exacerbated the "knee buckles," and it looked like he was bouncing up and down. I would never do this in front of others, but I wanted the student to see what he was doing, and it may not have been as obvious to him if I played the tape in real time.

We talked about his lack of gestures and mobility. I suggested that when he delivers his second briefing, I wanted him to work on **keeping his hands above his waist**, using open palms, which are more engaging. I told him to think of his upper body as being in a picture frame, and always try keeping his hands in the picture frame. If his hands are down at his sides, they are out of the picture frame. If you see anyone in a television commercial, marketing a product or service, you will hardly ever see them talking with their hands at their side. They will nearly always have their hands above their waist, openly engaging their audience with open palms.

The second thing I asked him to do in his second briefing was to be more mobile and less rigid. I suggested he move a bit when he begins to talk about each of his main points. This way he could keep his mobility subtly consistent with the structure of his briefing, and it will flow better and be more engaging. I also said that he needed to be careful not to "pace" back and forth almost predictably. If the audience can predict the mobility of the briefer by predicting his or her movement, then that would classify as pacing, in my opinion.

During his second briefing, the participant made a conscious effort to keep his hands above his waist, gestured a bit, and maintained a subtle mobility that was consistent with the structure of his briefing. I know those changes don't sound like much, but the difference between the first briefing and the second briefing was absolutely profound. When he saw his videotape after his second briefing, he was able to see the difference these small changes made. It was gratifying to him and me as well.

Disorganized Presentation

In many ways, it boils down to organization. When your briefing is organized, you feel much more comfortable because you have more control of the information. When you have more control of your information, you can be more focused on your delivery and your audience. Having a clear path to follow in your briefing can be very comforting. Think about how much more comforting it is to have a GPS in your car that shows the route, versus not knowing where you should turn next. Organization might be viewed as the GPS for your briefing (I know that's a bit corny, but it makes sense to me). Later in this chapter, I will provide two models for organizing your briefings. Before I do that, let's take a look at a **"Critical Path"** to consider when preparing an effective briefing.

Briefing "Critical Path"

As the Critical Path implies, the first step is to determine who your audience is and analyze their uniqueness. From there, you can define your purpose. Your purpose will be to either inform or persuade, or maybe a combination of both. After all, you still need to persuade your audience to accept your information. Once you've analyzed your audience and defined your purpose, you are now ready to organize your briefing in order to meet those goals. Later, I will provide two models to achieve both goals. When presenting your briefing, you must pay attention to adapting your language to the level of your audience and remember to use appropriate gestures, vocal intonation and eye contact. The next part of the Critical Path is making sure you are using the appropriate number of slides, following the 6x6 rule whenever possible, and using progressive disclosure of your bullets when appropriate.

Question & Answer Period (Q&A)

I've seen people give excellent briefings, but not do as well in the Q&A period. I've also seen people give mediocre briefings, and salvage them in the Q&A period. Essentially, the Q&A session can make you or break you. Here are a few things you might remember to do in the Q&A that may be helpful.

- **Anticipate Questions:** If you've done a good audience analysis and understand your purpose, you should be able to anticipate the types of questions you will likely be asked.

- **Acknowledge the Question/Questioner:** The principle of **acknowledgment** is particularly important here. Even when the question might be a bit challenging, it's usually a good idea to acknowledge the question or the person who asked it. You might say "Good question...," or "Good point...," or "Interesting question...." It's a good way to acknowledge and develop rapport with your audience.

- **Paraphrase the Question before answering:** It can be very embarrassing for the briefer who answers the wrong question, and the questioner lets him or her know about it in front of everyone. Before answering, it's useful to get in the habit of paraphrasing the question first to make sure you heard it correctly and understood it. You might say "Good question. Let me make sure I understand. You're asking...," or "Good point. If I understand correctly, you're asking...." It's also a subtle way of clarifying and verifying while acknowledging the question, as well as giving the briefer time to think about the answer. Additionally, it's also helpful in making sure everyone in the room heard the question.

- **Answer Briefly, Clearly and Directly (ABCD Rule):** After you've acknowledged and paraphrased the question (by the way, if the question is extremely obvious, and everyone heard it, you may not need to do this for every question), try to make your answer brief. It's best not to go on a tangent and get off topic. Be as clear as you can in your answer by dealing directly with the question, then moving on to the next question. I've seen people answer more than they need to, and the Q&A session goes spiraling off in another direction. There's one other thing I want to mention here. While you want to initially respond to the questioner, you also want to include the entire audience in your answer. When the briefer responds only to the questioner, and when the answer takes some time or is followed up by another question, the audience could be observing a dialogue between the questioner and the briefer. If the briefer limits his or her responses only to the questioner, the rest of the audience may feel like "potted plants," so include them in your responses.

- **Stay Cool, Be Personable, and Avoid Debates:** One of the biggest mistakes a briefer can make in the Q&A is to become defensive and argue with the questioner. If the briefer doesn't have an answer to the question, then he or she should say so, and tell the questioner the answer will be forthcoming. When briefers try to "fudge" the answer, it will likely show. Sometimes people may ask a very challenging and potentially defense-engendering question. Don't get hooked. When you get defensive, it shows your vulnerability, and generally doesn't work well. A better way of responding is to acknowledge and paraphrase the question if necessary, and give a focused, brief answer. If the questioner persists, you might say that you can discuss it further after the briefing, or you might ask an "overhead" question to the entire group to see if they want to contribute to answering the question. After all, the questioner may have a legitimate concern that you may need to know about. Lastly, if you've done a good audience analysis, you may ask well-informed audience members for their ideas. You might say "Mary, you've had a good deal of experience in the area Jim is asking about. What do you think?" You might need to be careful here, because you don't want to put your colleague in an awkward situation, but if you think the person would be able to make a legitimate contribution, why not use them as a resource. There are no guarantees here, but some of these suggestions may help. Again, the Q&A can make you or break you, so you want to handle them well.

The last part of the Critical Path consists of the "intervening variables" that are unique to every briefing: your Personal Style, Personal Credibility, and Political Realities.

- **Personal Style:** If you can, before your briefing, mingle with the audience, engage in some "small talk," be personable and engaging with them. It's amazing how this can put you more at ease and can create a friendly demeanor and style that people appreciate and respect. Smile at your audience when appropriate. Engage with them. Thank them up front for taking the time to attend your briefing, and how they will benefit from your information. Be "interpersonal."

- **Credibility:** Remember, the more organized you are, the more in control you are of your information. The more personable and engaging you are with your audience, the more likely it is that your credibility will be enhanced.

- **Political Realities:** Another reality of organizational life is that there are always political issues at play. They could take the form of personality clashes, hidden agendas, power struggles, egos, strategic direction, etc. If you've done your homework in preparation, you will likely be aware of them and adapt appropriately. For example, you might be addressing a group of upper-level managers, but in reality, you are really addressing the decision-maker. Don't make the mistake of maintaining eye contact with that person only. Be sure to address everyone in the room. There will likely be a few egos wanting attention, and they   could very well influence the outcome or decision. Briefings are political arenas, and your credibility is always on display and on the line. Remember: You're only as good as your last briefing!

At this point, I will present two Briefing Models that you may find useful. The first model shows how to organize an Informative Briefing. The second model shows how you might organize a Persuasive Briefing, in which you must identify a problem and its cause, propose a workable plan, and end by explaining the benefits of your proposed plan. Let's first look at the Informative Briefing Model.

Informative Briefing Model

(Introduction, Body & Conclusion)

Introduction
- Introduce Self/Organization
- Acknowledge Audience
- State Purpose
- Stess Importance of Topic
- Give Overview of Main Points

Body
- Present Main Points
- Support
- Internal Summary
- Transition
- (Repeat)

Conclusion
- Summary
- Reinforce your Purpose
- Final Comments
- Thank Audience
- Open to Q&A

Introduction

Let's take a closer look at the Informative Briefing Model. In the Introduction section, when it says to acknowledge your audience, you can let them know that you appreciate them taking the time to attend your briefing **(Acknowledgment).** That leads you directly into stating your purpose, by saying something like "The purpose of today's briefing is to...." After stating the purpose, it's usually a good idea to tell your audience why the information you are going to present is important to them in some way. In other words, you are telling them why they should listen to what you have to say, because it will be of some benefit to them **(Intentions).** From there, you show an Overview slide, which shows the main points you intend to cover to accomplish your purpose **(Expectations).**

Body

In the Body of the briefing, you want to cover each main point, and support them with examples, explanations, statistics, literal and hypothetical illustrations and analogies.

Illustrations are powerful rhetorical strategies. They are essentially short stories or examples of literal or hypothetical events. Let's say you are briefing your audience about the importance of computer security. The literal illustration might be based on an actual security incident that occurred, so you might say "Last month, the organization experienced a serious security breach that caused the following problems...." On the other hand, a hypothetical illustration is based on an incident that hasn't happened, but it could. In this case, you might say "Let's consider the following scenario. What if...." In both examples, you can heighten the attention of the audience by using illustrations that are relevant to them.

Analogies are particularly useful when you want to explain something technical to a relatively non-technical audience. As you know, an analogy is a comparison of two dissimilar things that possess similar characteristics. Let's say you are trying to describe and explain what a computer's "motherboard" is to a non-technical audience. In this scenario, you might say "The motherboard is like the engine in a car. The engine is the inner workings of the car that runs it, and the motherboard is the inner workings of the computer that runs it." Whenever we want to explain technical information to a non-technical audience, the use of analogies can be very helpful because they allow the audience members to relate to something they are familiar with. Consequently, they can better understand the technical information.

After you've stated your main point and supported it with effective supporting materials, you want to get in the habit of doing something that is far more important than it seems. Before you go to your next main point, briefly summarize your point and then transition to your next point. These are called "internal summaries," and in my opinion, they are critical in keeping your audience with you. Essentially, an internal summary tells the audience "This is where I've been, and this is where I intend to go. Come along with me...." You don't actually say that, but that's the intent of the internal summaries and transitions. It might sound like this. "Now that we've taken a look at... let's take a look at...." Here's a little formula to use when considering how to utilize internal summaries and transitions.

Main Points, Internal Summaries & Transitions Formula (IS&T Formula)

<u>STATE</u> the Main Point:

- "The first (second, third) point is..."
- "Another important point is..."

SUPPORT the Main Point with verbal materials:

- "Let's look at the following example..."
- "The following are some statistics representing..."
- "And by that, I mean..."
- "The term_____refers to..."
- "The following incident is an illustration of..."

SUMMARIZE the Main Point:

- "So, we can see that..."
- "To summarize up to this point..."

TRANSITION between Main Points:

- Now that we've looked at_____let's take a look at..."
- "So, we can see there's a problem. What can we do about..."

The **IS&T Formula** will help you tie your ideas together and allows the audience to follow you more easily.

Conclusion

In the Conclusion of the Informative briefing, you always want to summarize your main points, and reinforce your purpose. It's generally not a good idea to include any new information in your Summary. Keep your conclusion focused on your main purpose, and if possible, remind your audience how and why your information can be beneficial for them. You can create an almost generic way of concluding an Informative briefing by saying something like this. "I hope you've found this information useful, and that you now have a better understanding of......I'll be happy at this time, to answer any questions you might have." That type of statement in your conclusion generally works. You can also thank your audience for their time and invite them to ask any questions. **(Expectations,**

Acknowledgment, Intentions)

The next time you need to conduct an informative briefing or presentation, please try using the Model to develop your briefing. If you follow it, you're almost forced to be organized, and if you are organized, you will feel more comfortable, and if you feel more comfortable, you'll be more engaging with your audience, and you'll do great!

The Persuasive Briefing Model

The second type of model is the Persuasive Briefing Model. You might need to give this type of briefing when you want to get support for a new process or propose a more efficient way to do something. In these situations, there's often a need for a change, and your job would be to make recommendations for improvement. The structure is essentially based on the establishment of a problem, identifying the cause of the problem, recommending a plan or proposal that will eliminate the problem, and finally showing that your proposal will lead to significant benefits or advantages over the present system.

Usually, people need to give these types of briefings more often as they increase their technical and professional expertise. They can also be more challenging because the briefer is essentially asking to change the status quo, and people are often against change if it upsets their routine or comfort zone. The Q&A may also be more challenging since your proposal may affect the standard operating procedures that people have become used to. Let's take a look at the Persuasive Model to see how these types of briefings can be structured.

The Persuasive Briefing Model

(Problem, Cause, Proposal, Benefits)

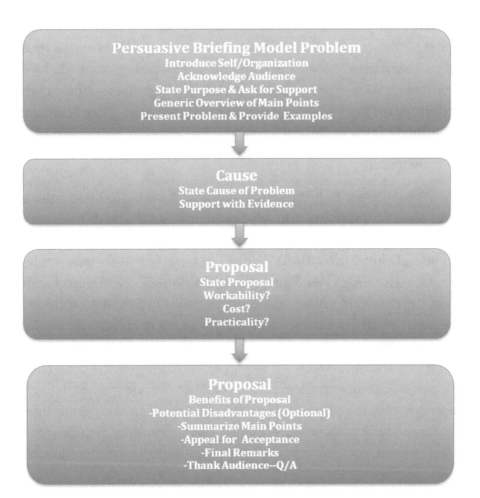

Persuasive Briefing Model Problem
Introduce Self/Organization
Acknowledge Audience
State Purpose & Ask for Support
Generic Overview of Main Points
Present Problem & Provide Examples

Cause
State Cause of Problem
Support with Evidence

Proposal
State Proposal
Workability?
Cost?
Practicality?

Proposal
Benefits of Proposal
-Potential Disadvantages (Optional)
-Summarize Main Points
-Appeal for Acceptance
-Final Remarks
-Thank Audience--Q/A

Introduction

Many of the same rhetorical elements used in the Informative Briefing can be used in the Persuasive Briefing. You will still introduce yourself, your organization, and acknowledge your audience. Be careful how you state your Purpose, however. You want to persuade your audience to take an action or change their views on something, but you don't want to tell them that your purpose is to "persuade" them. Instead, you might want to say that you appreciate their expertise, and you are seeking their support in the resolution of a problem or issue that impacts them. **(Expectations, Acknowledgment, Intentions)**

Overview

When I refer to a "Generic Overview," I mean that you don't go into specific detail here. Instead, you provide the path you intend to take in the briefing. You might say something like this. **(Setting Expectations & Intention)** "Today, I'm going to talk about a problem we have been experiencing with…. Additionally, I will describe the root cause of this problem, and propose a solution that I think will resolve this issue. Finally, I will show that my proposal will provide us with significant benefits over the present situation. I know this is an important issue for all of us. **(Acknowledgment)** Let's take a closer look at this problem…." This generic overview doesn't go into detail; it sets the stage for the path you intend to take. From there, you provide examples and evidence that support the significance of the problem, and that it warrants the audience's consideration.

Cause

Once you've described the problem and its significance, you need to articulate what you consider the causes of the problem to be. Eventually leading to what you consider to be the root cause. Being able to identify a cause-and-effect relationship is extremely important at this stage of the briefing. You must do this in order to justify your proposal later on. Be sure that at every stage of this briefing, you are able to support your views with data-based evidence.

Proposal

Now that you've identified the problem and its predominant cause, you're in a better position to internally summarize and transition to your Proposal. If you are briefing upper-level managers, I believe you must pay particular attention to the following three things. Is your Proposal "workable?" Is it "practical?" Is it "cost-effective?" That's what the managers will want to know. For example, you could propose a plan that will work, but it may not be practical because of its cost or difficulty to implement. You could also propose a plan that is very practical and cost-effective, but unfortunately, it may have only a short-term effect, and may not be workable or viable in the long term. Paying attention to workability, practicality and cost are very important considerations when proposing changes.

Benefits

Once you have identified the problem, cause and proposed a solution, you now want to show how your proposal will lead to significant benefits or advantages over the status quo. A question you might ask is whether you should present both advantages and disadvantages here. It's really up to you, but I lean in the direction of presenting both. By doing so, you are letting your audience know that you've done your homework, and that you are well versed in the topic. You can show that even though there may be some initial disadvantages, they are outweighed by the benefits or advantages your proposal offers.

Once you have developed these four elements, Problem, Cause, Proposal and Benefits, you will make a respectful final appeal to the audience to support your proposal, and you are now open for any questions they may have. **(Expectations, Acknowledgment, Intentions)**

I want to conclude by saying that both briefing models presented are not etched in stone. They are simply Guides that will help you be better organized and prepared to give an effective briefing whether you're attempting to inform or persuade your audience.

Chapter 11

Everyone's a Customer!

Years ago, customer service training was often called "Smile training." In today's world, customer service is viewed quite differently. As I've said before, most of the training and consulting work I've done over the years has been with the Department of Defense and Intelligence Community, where I assure you that customer service is very serious business. In fact, at times, disastrous outcomes can occur because of poor "service."

It's also serious business in the private sector as well. If a company doesn't take care of its customers, it could be quickly out of business. The more successful organizations understand that customers drive the business. They recognize that customers are not interruptions to the work. They are the **purpose** of it. If you were to examine the most successful companies about their quality philosophy, I would guess the first thing they would say is that they were "customer-driven" or "customer-focused."

There's a story about Jeff Bezos, founder of Amazon. As the story goes, when Bezos had meetings with his senior people to discuss important issues, an empty chair sat at the head of the conference table. This chair represented the "customer." When they discussed a new direction, a new service, process, etc., Bezos would often look to the empty chair and ask how the topic of their discussion would affect the customer. True or not, that story epitomizes an organization that is **"customer-driven"** and **"customer-focused."** Every decision that is made or any new service that's provided must always have the customer in mind. After all, the customer is what keeps organizations in business.

The second characteristic of a successful company's quality philosophy is that they are "**process-oriented.**" They continually look at their processes to see what's working and what isn't. Also, they constantly work to **improve on those processes**, by **empowering** those employees closest to the operational level.

So, there you have it. I'm suggesting that successful organizations focus on the following characteristics:

- **Customer-Driven & Customer-Focused**

- **Process-Oriented**

- **Constant Improvement**

- **Empowered Workforce**

Successful, customer driven and customer-focused organizations look at **everyone** as a customer. When people think of customers, they may tend to think of them as external to an organization. They are the people that buy or use the organization's services and products. The focus on external customers only, is insufficient because not enough attention might be given to **internal** customers. They are the ones who really make it all work by providing those services and products.

It's useful to consider customers in two ways. The first is the **Process Customer**. The Process Customer is anyone who is down-line or up-line from the work being performed. The Process Customer is the next person who adds value, and they could be internal or external. In fact, they could be your coworkers. For example, let's assume you work in a team of three people, and you receive a database that needs to be presented in a briefing to upper management. You hand the database off to Karen, your coworker, who will add some explanatory text to it so that it is more readable and more easily interpreted. Your coworker, Karen, is actually your Process Customer. She has taken your database and added value by making it easier to interpret. Karen then hands the database with text to James, who adds some graphics to the text and database to increase its readability and clarity. James is now Karen's Process Customer by adding even more value to the document. Lastly, James hands off the database, text and graphics back to you to finalize and brief to upper management. You guessed it. You are James' Process Customer. In other words, we are all customers to one another. If one team member drops the ball, it can make the whole team look bad. Additionally, if one person doesn't do his or her part, it can undermine the whole fabric of the team. Management won't ask who did what. They will likely say your **group** messed up. Finally, if this happens, it is likely the team members may say "Wait a minute. I did my part! Someone else dropped the ball, and they made us all look bad!" This is not good for team morale. Another reality of organizational life is that if you don't take care of your process customers by doing your part in a process, then no one wins.

The second type of customer is the **Ultimate Customer.** The Ultimate Customer is the end user of your product or service. One of the challenges organizations have in meeting Ultimate Customer requirements is to understand, meet, and exceed the customer's **expectations**. Sometimes, the Ultimate Customer's expectations may be unrealistic, especially when they don't understand your processes or what needs to be done to meet their requirement. Consequently, the more you can **educate** the Ultimate Customer about your processes, including how and what will be done to meet the requirement, the more flexible Ultimate Customers tend to be. For example, what if you have an Ultimate Customer who is dissatisfied with the amount of time it will take for you to perform a service or deliver a product? Sometimes the dissatisfaction is a function of not understanding what they are asking of you, and what you need to do to meet their needs. You may lessen this dissatisfaction by saying something like "I understand how frustrating this must be for you" **(Reflecting and Acknowledging feelings).** "I want to do whatever needs to be done to get the product to you" **(Intentions).** "Our process in getting the product delivered is in three phases, and each phase takes approximately this much time" **(Educate the customer**

on the process). "I will do everything I can to expedite things on our end, to see if we can get that product to you by tomorrow" **(Expectation)**. When you educate the Ultimate Customer about your processes, they will usually have a better understanding of what they are asking of you, and better appreciate what you are doing for them. They may even say something like this: "I didn't realize you had to go through all that. Thanks for letting me know you'll do what you can to get the product delivered." Now, I'm not so naïve to think that will always happen. I can say however, that it is more likely to happen if you remember the **"3 Things,"** and educate your customer on your process.

Lastly, please be careful not to promise what you won't be able to deliver. Make sure your other Process Customers are willing and able to perform, in order to deliver what you promised. For that matter, it's no different if it's a process or ultimate customer, a spouse, friend, son or daughter, or neighbor. If you promise something that you really can't control, you run the risk of creating more problems. So, make sure you control the process, and can do what you said you will do, before you make promises.

Customer Expectations

The interesting thing about expectations is that you must constantly manage them. Let's say you have a customer (Process or Ultimate) who has expectations about a deliverable's timeline. You pull your team together, and everyone does a great job. Things seem to come together, and in fact, you exceed the customer's expectations. That's great, isn't it? You always want to exceed customer expectations, don't you? Well, yes, but you still need to manage them, because by exceeding the customer's expectations, you have now "raised the bar." If you and your team had to put in an extraordinary amount of effort to meet the customer's requirement, and it's not something you can do on a regular basis, then you had better have a discussion with your customer to clarify that in the future, certain things need to be done before requirements can be met. If you don't have this discussion, the next time you attempt to meet the customer's requirement, you may hear "What do you mean you can't do it by .... You were able to do it last time!" I think we should always try to exceed customer expectations, but must also remember that by exceeding them, you have now raised the bar for the next time you deal with the customer. So, you need to manage them.

Quality customer service is not always an easy thing to measure. However, research conducted at Texas A&M suggests there are five dimensions of quality service that can be applied to any organization. These five dimensions can be described by the acronym RATER:

- **Reliability:** The ability to provide what was promised, dependably and accurately

- **Assurance:** The knowledge and courtesy of employees; the ability to convey trust and confidence

- **Tangibles:** Physical facilities, equipment, appearance of personnel

- **Empathy:** Degree of caring and individual attention provided

- **Responsiveness:** Willingness to help customers and provide prompt service

If you look at these characteristics of quality service, you can see how **Expectations, Acknowledgement** and **Intentions** play a part. Paying attention to the quality service dimensions can help any organization better meet customer requirements.

Once again, let me reiterate that in our interpersonal lives at home and elsewhere, isn't it important to be reliable; keep promises; be courteous and caring? Isn't it also important to convey trust and confidence in the people we care about; acknowledge others; attend to their needs, and be helpful and prompt in doing what we say we will do? Aren't these characteristics also representative of effective interpersonal relationships?

Dealing with an Angry or Frustrated Customer

We've likely been in situations when we were the frustrated or angry customer, or we have had to deal with a frustrated or angry customer in our jobs. How should you respond to Process and Ultimate Customers when they are upset for whatever reason? Here are a few steps you might consider in handling these types of situations.

Dealing with a Frustrated or Angry Customer

- Deal with the person's feelings—empathize

- Ask questions—open, clarifying, closed (ask for permission)

- Paraphrase/summarize the problem/situation

- Deal with the problem by:

    o Finding out what the customer actually wants or needs

    o If you can't give them what they need, suggest alternatives

    o Share information on procedures if appropriate

    o Agree and summarize a solution

    o Follow up: do what you say you will do!

Let's take a closer look at the steps. If someone is frustrated or angry, before doing anything else, it's important to acknowledge those feelings by reflecting on them ("I can certainly understand how frustrating this must be for you"). At this point, you also want to let them know you want to do what is necessary to resolve their issue (Intention), and that you will do everything you can to resolve the problem. (Expectation)

After you've acknowledged and empathized with the person's feelings, you want to ask them some questions. However, before asking your questions, it's useful to **ask for permission** first. There's a reason for asking permission. When people feel frustrated or angry, they also feel out of control. Asking for permission to ask a question tends to give the person a psychological feeling of being in control. The very act of asking for permission suggests to the other person that he or she is in control. Otherwise, how could they give you permission if they weren't in control? It's a subtle way of acknowledging and respecting the other person and it's amazing how it works.

Once you've asked questions and have a better idea about the problem, you want to clarify and verify by **paraphrasing** your understanding of the problem or situation. Once you get agreement on the problem, you'll be in a better position to deal with it.

At this point, you want to make sure you know exactly what the person needs. Sometimes customers may **want** something they **don't need** or **need** something they **don't want**. Additionally, you may not always be able to give them what they want or need, and you may have to suggest alternatives if that's appropriate or possible. You may also need to share information on your process for them to better understand what they are asking of you, and what you intend to do to help meet their requirement.

Before ending the interaction, it's a good idea for you to paraphrase and summarize what both you and the customer will do or expect from one another. This helps to clarify and verify the understanding from this point forward. (**Expectations and Intentions**)

Thank the customer for their understanding and willingness to work with you to resolve the issue, and, if appropriate, follow up to see how things went. (**Acknowledgment**)

A few years ago, I was working with a large telecommunication company's IT group, and we developed a set of "service principles" that the workforce was asked to adhere to. The IT segment of the telecommunication company was embedded in a large government agency, and it was crucial for the company to manage internal relations with the agency's workforce. It was also decided that we use the term "mission partners" rather than customers, because the organization's leadership felt that term more precisely defined the nature of the relationship. Even though the focus of these service principles is on information technology, I thought it would still be useful to share some of these principles, with the hope you will find them helpful. The following represents a sample of those principles:

Exceptional Service Principles

In order to effectively meet requirements, we must resolutely follow these Service Principles:

Make Every Interaction with Mission Partners Beneficial

- Make the experience positive and purposeful for all parties

- Make sure the engagement is result-driven, including appropriate follow-up

- Take ownership to help mission partners resolve the issues

- If you're not empowered to do so, provide feedback on who will take ownership—make sure the handoff takes place

- Honor your commitments to your mission partners

Demonstrate Expertise and Share Information about Policies and Procedures

- All of our employees must demonstrate enough expertise and knowledge of policies to help mission partners, rather than use policies and procedures as an excuse to say "no"

- Take the time with mission partners to ensure they have been helped

- Show knowledge of business practices and our overall organizations

- Manage mission partner expectations to understand timelines for feedback and follow-up

- Stay current on policies, procedures, and the overall IT environment

Build and Maintain Teamwork with our Mission Partners

- Know your mission partners and their mission

- Don't be afraid to ask questions

- Anticipate the mission partners' needs

- Collaborate and include mission partners in planning and decision-making

- Ensure you have coordinated with other business partners before making promises to the mission partner

Foster the Internal Team

- Treat every team member as a mission partner

- Work across "stove-pipes" within IT organizations and other service providers

- Learn to have effective technical exchange meetings
- Share information among team members
- Ensure smooth hand-offs that are transparent to the mission partner
- Do not speak ill of partners and partner organizations
- Honor your commitments made to or by your partner teams
- Acknowledge and honor partners in peer organizations with positive recognition

Provide a Supportive Management Environment

- Challenge, empower and support the team to succeed
- Endorse, support, and follow formal management training guidelines
- Lead by example
- "Work yourself out of a job" (develop and challenge your employees to take over and move to the next level; support and allow them to make decisions)

Establish and Support a Continuous Learning Environment

- Support formal training programs: technical, managerial, programmatic and leadership training
- Review training needs and gaps
- Teach people the processes behind the tools
- Share lessons learned
- Wherever possible, provide training opportunities to align with career development

- Incorporate expectations in contracts to invest in training for employees to match future technology needs and trends

- Plan staff training to meet future technology needs and trends

- All IT professionals need to have mission partner service training

Identify Opportunities for More Efficient and Effective Service

- Measure progress and make appropriate adjustments

- Every activity is an opportunity for improvement in service

- Look for feedback for efficiencies and improved effectiveness

- Expect and encourage feedback for improvement among your own workforce and your mission partners

- The IT organizations should provide mechanisms to evaluate, and as appropriate, implement the recommendations and provide feedback

Effectively managing process and ultimate customer service requirements represents the "lifeblood" of organizations. It's important to adhere to the above Principles, and to remember that we are all customers to one another. Hopefully, the skills discussed in this chapter will help. Finally, don't forget that the customer service skills discussed in this chapter, have direct application to all of our interpersonal relationships at work and at home. Considering and practicing the **"3 Things"** while interacting with others can pay real benefits in keeping our conversations respectful and productive.

Final Comments

Communication is a complex, dynamic process, and can be quite difficult to master. In fact, it is imperfect. It's sort of like golf. You'll do well some days and not so well on others, but you know you have to keep working at it. Hopefully, this book will be helpful for us to keep working at it, by making us better communicators at work and at home.

Understanding and making an effort to master the **"3 Things"** really can make all the difference in the way we manage our relationships both professionally and personally. I know, because over the years, I've struggled with these three things, and still make more than my share of mistakes. However, I continue to work at it (as well as my golf game!).

It is my sincere hope that the recommendations provided in this book will be helpful to you in various aspects of your lives. My very best to all of you while you're on that journey.

The following **Appendices** consist of some useful exercises to augment the topics and skills discussed in this book. All of the answers to the exercises are characterized as "recommended" answers. They are not designed to be "right" or "wrong." You may not agree with all of the recommendations, and that's okay. The recommendations are designed to give insight and provoke thought about how to deal with real-life situations that require effective communication

Appendix A: Active Listening Exercise

Appendix B: Role Plays in Giving Feedback & Active Listening

Appendix C: Problem Ownership Exercise

Appendix D: Conducting a Problem-Solving-Decision-Making Meeting Exercise

Appendix A
Active Listening Exercise

Below are some examples where active listening responses can be used. Put yourself in each of these situations as if you were being talked to. For each of the situations, you will have five possible responses. Circle any **two** responses that would represent how you might actually respond in that situation. If you don't think any of the responses are representative of the way you would respond, please force yourself to choose the two that come closest to the way you might respond.

Situation #1:

Six weeks ago, you hired a new employee. She has been slow to catch on to a particular phase of the job. You have had a senior employee working with her to improve her skills. One day, you walk by her workstation, and ask her how she is doing. She says, "To tell you the truth, not too well. I don't know if I'm going to make it. How do you do this?"

You reply:

    a. "Here, let me show you. These things can be tricky."

    b. "You sound pretty worried about how you're doing."

    c. "Don't worry about it. I'm sure you'll get the hang of it."

    d. "I know you want to get this right."

    e. "Why don't you get Mary to show you again? She's been helping you, and I think it's best to stick with one person while you are learning something."

Situation #2:

In order for your area to function well, it's necessary to coordinate your efforts with those of a coworker from another area. You're in your office, setting up the next week's work schedule when Bob Jones, the coworker from the other area, comes charging into the office without knocking, and says, "Listen! I'm tired of having to clean up your mistakes. When are you going to do your job right? Enough is enough!"

You reply:

    a. "Calm down Bob. We're not going to get anywhere yelling at one another."

    b. "Listen. Don't you ever come barging into my office like this again. I won't put up with that kind of behavior from anyone!"

    c. "You sound really angry, Bob."

    d. "Okay, sit down and let's talk about it. I'm sure we can work it out."

    e. "I know you're upset Bob. What's happened?"

Situation #3:

One of your peers has been bypassed for a promotion. You are having lunch with him, just after he has been told someone else has gotten the job he wanted. He says, "I can't believe it! That's what hard work will do for you. Break your back for five years, and the job goes to someone else. I've had it with this place."

You reply:

    a. "It must be really frustrating for you."

    b. "I know what you mean. I had the same thing happen to me at the place I worked before."

    c.   "Well, you know how it is in the bureaucracy; to get along, you have to go along."

    d.   "You ought to give yourself a day to cool down before you do something you'll regret. Don't forget; you'll lose a lot of benefits if you quit."

    e.   "It must make you wonder what it takes to get ahead in the organization."

Situation #4:

You are a Branch Head in the HR Division. The Head of another Branch calls to talk to you about one of your staffing specialists. He says, "Your man, Bill, is not coming through for us. He keeps sending us people to interview who just can't cut it. If we don't fill the position soon, we're going to fall way behind. That's the last thing I need."

You reply:

    a.   "Sorry to hear that. I'll have a talk with Bill and get it straightened out right away."

    b.   "Sounds as if Bill's not sending the people with the right qualifications."

    c.   "Are you sure you made it clear to Bill the kind of people you were looking for?"

    d.   "So, you're dissatisfied with the people Bill has been sending you, and you're concerned you'll get behind if you don't hire someone soon."

    e.   "I think it would be best if you discussed this directly with Bill. I'll call him for you."

Situation #5:

You've been working on a major project. In order for you to complete your work on time, it is necessary for another project team member to give you vital information by the end of the day. The fellow team member has assured you in writing that the work will be done on time. It's 4:55 p.m., and you haven't received the needed information. You walk over to his desk and say, "I'm concerned about not getting the information I need from you because..." Before you can finish the sentence, he says, "Well, if I had gotten the information I needed from HR on time, I wouldn't have been late!"

You reply:

    a.   "So, HR didn't come through for you?"

    b.   "You and I both know we discussed the date thoroughly before you committed to it."

    c.   "Why didn't you tell me before now that HR wasn't getting you your information?"

    d.   "Let's see. You set the date to appease me and you're upset about not getting good service from HR.."

    e.   "I would appreciate you letting me finish my sentence before you interrupt. That's a bad habit you have. It may be why you didn't get what you needed from the HR.."

Situation #6:

You supervise a department of ten people. One of your most productive employees is a single woman named Mary. One day, Jim, another excellent employee, comes in to talk to you. He says, "Have you noticed how much time Mary spends talking with everyone all over the building? She should be working instead of spending all her time socializing. She thinks just because she works fast, she can goof off when she wants. It's not fair to the rest of us."

You reply:

    a.   "Sounds like you and the other employees feel jealous of Mary."

   b.   "So, when Mary talks to other employees, you feel irritated because you think she should be working instead?"

   c.   "You don't think Mary is doing a good job?"

   d.   "So, you believe it's unfair for Mary to goof off just because she's a fast worker."

   e.   "To tell you the truth, Jim, when I look at Mary's work record compared to most of the other employees, I wish you would all spend time "socializing." It might improve the productivity around here."

Situation #7:

For the past few days, several of you have noticed that Jane, a coworker, has looked very tired and has not talked very much to anyone. This is unusual for Jane. You see her in the cafeteria having coffee and decide to sit down with her. You say, "Jane, you've looked worried the past few days. Do you want to talk about it?" She says, "No, I'd rather not."

You reply:

   a.   "You really should, you know. It's not good to keep these things bottled up inside you."

   b.   "If you change your mind, I'm always willing to let you bend my ear."

   c.   "I'm sorry! I was just trying to be helpful."

   d.   "Okay."

   e.   "You should at least go see the nurse."

Situation #8:

One of your peers has just received an offer from another organization. He comes to your office to tell you about it. He says, "I don't know what to do. It's a great offer, but it means moving, and my wife and kids are happy here. I feel as if I have a good future with the organization, but you never know about these things. It's a tough choice. What would you do?

You reply:

    a. "I've always believed you have to take a good offer when it comes. Besides, statistics still show that those who change organizations move up faster and earn more."

    b. "I really don't know. You're the one who has to live with the decision."

    c. "Sounds like you're torn between the two options."

    d. "Have you talked with the boss about it yet? She might sweeten the pot to get you to stay."

    e. "It is a tough choice, and it must be difficult deciding what to do."

Situation #9:

A colleague has been working several weeks on a major assignment. You used to have the same job he now holds. While you and he are having lunch, he says, "This assignment has been going well up to this point, but now I'm stuck. I have several ways to go, and I'm not sure which one is best. I'd sure hate to mess up. Have you any advice from your experience?"

You Reply:

    a. "Not really."

    b. "Let's go to my office after lunch. I'm sure we can figure it out together."

    c. "No, but I believe you'll make a good choice. Your judgment has always been good in the past."

d. "Sounds like you feel uncertain about which way to go and are concerned you might blow it."

e. "You seem to have several options and it's difficult to decide which one is best."

Situation #10:

You and a business colleague are having a working dinner on the third night of your trip together. He looks depressed, and you ask him if anything is wrong. He says, "It's my wife. I just talked to her on the phone, and she was complaining about my being gone all the time. I guess I have been on the road more than I thought. She told me if things don't change soon, she'll seek a separation."

You reply:

a. "I'm sorry to hear that. I'm sure things will work out, though. She probably had a bad day."

b. "Doesn't she understand that all these trips you take are the reason the family is so well off?"

c. "Your wife wants you home more, and she's thinking about separating?"

d. "I know just how you feel. It's tough keeping our spouses happy these days."

e. "Sounds like you're really worried about this."

Scoring Sheet

Transfer your answers from the test to the appropriate column below (a, b, c, d, e) and circle the number shown in that column (2, 4, 6). Then add the two numbers together in each situation and put the total number in the far right-hand column and place your total in the box. Your score should fall between 40 and 100.

	(a)	(b)	(c)	(d)	(e)	Total Score
Situation #1	2	6	2	4	2	
Situation #2	2	2	4	2	6	
Situation #3	6	2	2	2	4	
Situation #4	2	4	2	6	2	
Situation #5	4	2	2	6	2	
Situation #6	2	6	2	4	2	
Situation #7	2	4	2	6	2	
Situation #8	2	2	6	2	4	
Situation #9	2	2	2	6	4	
Situation #10	2	2	4	2	6	

Total Score=

(40-60) may indicate difficulty hearing both content and feelings. Initial reaction tends to be to the situation/problem not the person.

(60-80) may indicate a tendency to focus on either the content or the feelings, but not necessarily both.

(80-100) indicates a strong amount of listening skill. You are probably quite good at picking up both the verbal and nonverbal messages.

**I don't expect agreement with all of the recommended answers, or maybe they weren't worded the way you think they should have been. The exercise is designed to give you some insight into what paraphrasing, reflecting and probing might sound like.

Appendix B

Role-Plays in Giving Feedback & Active Listening

Pick a friend or trusted colleague. Role-play these scenarios. Give each other feedback on how they went. (Some situations require you to use the SBIS steps; with others, you should be an active listener.)

Situation 1:

You're exasperated. Your administrative assistant just presented to you for your signature, the sixth consecutive piece of outgoing correspondence containing numerous typographical and grammatical errors. Some of these errors cannot be remedied by a spell or grammar checker. You decide to talk to your assistant...

Situation 2:

Terry, your direct report, has been consistently late for the last two weeks. This lateness seems to be a pattern since you've talked to John about this problem before, and Terry agreed to be more punctual. The problem has apparently surfaced again. You decide to talk to Terry...

Situation 3:

The organization has recently decided to standardize some of its database applications. Most of the employees are making the transition. Shawn, one of your direct reports whom you feel could have a bright future, is absolutely against one of the new applications. You feel Shawn's unwillingness to learn the new app is not only affecting the department's productivity but will also limit Shawn's career opportunities and upward mobility. You decide to talk to Shawn...

Situation 4:

Chris, a member of the project you manage, has been, over the last month, consistently turning in work late. The lateness has caused other members of the team to fall behind in their due dates since they can't start their phase of the operation until they receive the completed work from Chris. You decide to talk to Chris...

Situation 5:

Pat, a person you've been mentoring, has an opportunity to move to another department. The move holds considerable opportunities for Pat. However, the person Pat will report to has a relatively autocratic style that Pat tends to dislike. Essentially, the move would be career-enhancing for Pat, but may not be worth the stress of working with someone whose style is difficult for Pat to deal with. You decide to talk to Pat...

Situation 6:

All of the position descriptions (PD) have been greatly modified. Some of them involve major changes in qualifications. Your employee got matched against a PD that implies less status and, perhaps in the long term, less money. Your employee has done a good, steady job up to now, consistently getting awards and salary increases. You are about to discuss this issue with your employee.

Situation 7:

Your employee is part of a position description (PD) that has been identified as one that will gradually phase out. Your employee has the option of staying as is or greatly re-skilling to land in a PD that has some kind of a future left with it. You are about to discuss this issue with your employee.

Situation 8:

You're working with an employee on his/her Individual Development Plan (IDP) and Career Training Plan. This employee hates to go to any type of training. You strongly feel this attitude will have a significant negative impact on the person's career.

Situation 9:

Your employee has just found out he/she wasn't promoted, and states that it was their understanding that unless you "screw up," you automatically get promoted. You want to discuss this issue with your employee.

Situation 10:

Your son/daughter has been spending time with friends who you feel are a bad influence. You decide you want to talk to your son/daughter about your concerns.

Situation 11:

It's time for your son/daughter to make a decision about what college to attend. You would like for him/her to attend a smaller university because it will provide more personalized attention. Your son/daughter wants to go to a large university across the country. You decide to talk about it.

Situation 12:

Your spouse has an important meeting scheduled. At the meeting, your spouse will be recommending, in a briefing to upper-level managers, a new procedure that should improve efficiency. However, some of the managers are concerned the new procedure will reduce their influence and span of control. Your spouse asks for your advice on the issue.

Write Your Own Situation...

Appendix C

Problem Ownership Exercise

The following cases are designed to test your ability to identify who has "ownership" of a problem in various situations. Read each case carefully and place a ✓ in the appropriate column on the scoring sheet.

Put yourself in each of the eleven situations. Read each situation thoroughly, and then place a √ in the **"You Own the Problem"** column if you feel you would have the concern in the situation. Place a √ in the **"Others Own the Problem"** column if you believe one or more individuals (other than yourself, of course) have ownership of the problem in the situation. Place a √ in the **"Group Owns the Problem"** column if you believe two or more people, **including you** have ownership of the problem in the situation. In other words, you are included in the group. Finally, place a √ in **"No One Owns the Problem"** if you don't think there is a problem. Make only one choice per case description.

**Please note: Remember that these situations are fluid and could change in seconds. When reading each situation, ask yourself, "At this moment, based on the information available, who owns the problem?"

Problem Ownership Scoring Sheet

Case	You Own the Problem	Others Own the Problem	Group Owns the Problem	No One Owns the Problem
Case #1				
Case #2				
Case #3				
Case #4				
Case #5				
Case #6				
Case #7				
Case #8				
Case #9				
Case #10				
Case #11				

CASE #1

You have a boss who, for some unexplained reason, has rules about the amount of time the employees in his department take for lunch. In your organization, the time allotted is thirty minutes, and your boss has his secretary check periodically to be sure his people are staying within the limits.

One day you've been at lunch for just about thirty minutes. As you are getting up to leave, Craig Baker from Purchasing sits down at your table. You don't want to be impolite and leave Craig alone, so you stay and talk with him until someone else sits down about fifteen minutes later. You also take advantage of your time with Craig to discuss the prices and types of mobile devices available. On the previous day, you had just received organizational approval to purchase a new iPhone or something similar.

That afternoon, your boss calls you into his office. Without asking for any explanation, he reminds you of the thirty-minute policy for lunch. He smiles and says he appreciates your understanding, and he ends the conversation by turning to take a phone call.

CASE #2

You are an administrator of the Internal Services Department in an organization with offices in several states. A number of these offices are in small towns and are run by men in their fifties, some with twenty or more years in the organization, and many of them can be a bit "rough around the edges." Your department does a great deal of work with these men. You have received permission to add one person to your staff. The person you hire will have to travel extensively and will spend much of his/her time working directly with the small-town offices.

One day Nancy Hughes, a young woman from another department, asks to talk with you. When she arrives at your office, she begins by saying she has heard through the grapevine that you have an opening. She indicates that she would be very interested in the position.

Because you like her as a person, and want to be helpful, and mentor her, you tell her that even though she is qualified, you are reluctant to place her in that position. You explain that the job involves extensive travel and a great deal of work with the small-town offices. You say you just do not believe that the veterans in those offices would ever give her a chance, and that you are not willing to take the risk or put her in such a difficult position. When you finish, Nancy expresses surprise that you would say such things and exits red-faced.

CASE #3

It is time for your annual raise. You and your boss have gone over your objectives every two months during the past year. You have met or exceeded all of the goals which you could control and have accomplished several other objectives in addition to your defined objectives. You are aware that the average allotment for raises in the organization for the current fiscal year is eight percent. When your boss, Sam Hardy, reveals that your raise is six percent, you are very surprised and even shocked. When you ask why, he says he thought you deserved more but that he was vetoed by his boss, Mort Harvey. It seems Mort had heard a rumor that you came to work late quite often a few months back. He started checking on you and found the rumor to be true.

What Mort did not know was that you had been working on a project with someone in another division and, because he was located in another building between your home and your office location, you had been spending the first thirty minutes to an hour at his office. As your immediate boss, Sam Hardy knew where you were, and you felt you had met your reporting obligations.

CASE #4

Your organization has season tickets to professional basketball games. Four weeks ago, you arranged for the Human Resources Department, which is responsible for ticket distribution, to get you four tickets to this evening's game. You have plans to entertain the district sales manager of a major supplier. You believe there is going to be a shortage of the supplier's product in the coming months, and you want to use the opportunity to maintain goodwill and your preferred customer status. You believe tonight will be a big help because the sales manager is a basketball fan and has mentioned several times that he is looking forward to the game.

At four p.m. the day of the game, you get a call from Harry Jones in the Human Resources Department. He tells you he is sorry but that he will not be able to give you tickets for this evening's game.

He says the vice-president, to whom Human Resources reports, called and asked for tickets because some close friends of his are in town. Before Harry checked the reservations list, he told the vice-president he could have the tickets. Harry again says he's sorry, but you will have to take a rain check.

CASE #5

For the last week or so, you have been thinking about having a conference with Ray Walsh, one of the people who reports to you. He has been working with you for about nine months. Ray started out very well, and after six months you gave him a five percent raise. His raise would have been higher, but you were restricted by organizational policy.

Lately, however, Ray's performance has gone downhill. He has accomplished some goals, but he is now starting to fall behind in key areas. Through the grapevine, you are also aware that Ray was unhappy about his raise and your rejection of an idea for a product development change.

CASE #6

You have just arrived home from a hard day at the office. As a matter of fact, you have spent the last two hours of the day discussing a difficult problem. A major proposal you have presented is meeting resistance from another department in the organization; you and your boss have been trying to come up with ways to break down the resistance. Selling the proposal could be a big factor in your own career future. You are still up in the air about how to handle the situation.

As you kiss your spouse hello, you get very little response, which is quite unusual. You start to relate your afternoon's conversation with your boss. While you are talking, your spouse begins to browse through a magazine. You get the impression that your spouse has not heard a word you have said. Your spouse doesn't seem to care about your hard day at work.

CASE #7

You are taking a coffee break with some fellow employees. The conversation has covered the usual assortment of topics. Recently, a magazine article about the book **Dress for Success** has been circulated to all the men by one of the organization's executives. The conversation at coffee drifts into discussing the dress standards suggested in the article. One of the men at the table, Steve Smith, happens to be wearing a bright sport coat and an equally bright tie. One of the other men at the table, Glen Morrison, begins to tease Steve about his clothing. Several other people chime in, each giving Steve a hard time about his outfit. During the verbal banter, you can see Steve's neck turning red. His laughter seems strained.

CASE #8

You are driving on a business trip with three fellow employees: Jim Harrison, Wilson Bole and Jane Thomas. During the drive, the conversation turns to the recent hiring of a new Chief Executive Officer (CEO) at your organization. There has been an enormous amount of speculation about what changes in organizational structure the new CEO might make. The four of you represent three different areas of the organization. Naturally, each group would like to gain more clout as a result of any organizational changes. For more than an hour, the group carries on a lively debate about what should be done. Jim says, "How about grabbing a bite to eat?" Everyone says, "Great!"

CASE #9

You are a supervisor in the personnel area of your organization. You have an employee, Joan Brown, who has been working with you for six months. She has been developing into an excellent employee. The two of you are in your office discussing her first performance record. At the end of the review session, you summarize your good feelings about Joan's performance and then ask her if there is anything you can do to help her.

Hesitantly, she indicates that one thing has been bothering her. It seems that George Smalley, the division head of a very influential part of the organization, has been making advances to her. Joan is concerned because she is married and knows that Mr. Smalley is too. She also knows that because of his position, Mr. Smalley could stop her advancement.

CASE #10

Your organization has a strict policy against having food or drink in the work area. Customers often come through the facilities, and the top administrators are concerned about the organization's image.

The week before Christmas, you and some other employees decide to put on a big spread for December 23. Everyone is to bring a variety of snacks, and the group will pay for a ham. All the food will be laid out on a table in an empty office.

On the morning of December 23, two division heads come through your area to a meeting. They see the employees eating at their desks and notice the buffet set up in the usually vacant office. They each take a couple cookies, wish everyone happy holidays, and go on to their meeting.

CASE #11

You manage the mailroom in a large organization. You are also responsible for the company's duplicating equipment. Occasionally, you will have someone in your area teach someone from another department how to run a particular piece of equipment. You do this so they can use the equipment on weekends or at night if there's an emergency.

It is Monday morning. You are reading your emails when Bob Hesselman, a division head, comes to your office. He's quite angry. He says that, contrary to your promise, you had not taught his employee, Stan Smith, how to run the duplicating equipment last Friday.

Just prior to Bob's arrival at your office, you had read an email from Marianne Jones, a relatively new employee, that on Friday, she had taught Stan how to use the equipment, as instructed. You show the note to Bob, and he says that he doesn't care what it says. Stan was not taught how to use the equipment. He asks you what you are going to do about the situation.

Problem Ownership Exercise Score Sheet

**Five points for each recommended answer
Add up all of your answers that were recommended
in each column.**

Your total will give you a score from 0-55. Good luck!

You	Others	Group	No One
Case #	Case #	Case #	Case #
1	2	5	8
3	7	6	10
4	9	11	

Grand Total: _____

Appendix D

Conducting a Problem-Solving-Decision-Making Meeting Exercise

Assume you are a manager of a large department, and you have asked your first-line supervisors to attend a meeting to explore the problem of low productivity in the department. Your task is to come up with a decision(s) which effectively resolves the problem. Below are twelve situations which could happen in any meeting. As you read through each situation, you'll have a choice of three alternative actions to resolve the situation. Circle which action you feel would be most feasible for each situation.

Situation 1:

You've just finished stating the purpose of the meeting—to decide on a method to increase productivity in the department. What do you do now?

a. As leader, you should recommend a solution.

b. Try to find out which supervisor is to blame.

c. Define the nature of the problem in precise terms.

Situation 2:

You've defined the problem and asked if the members agree. You now want some of their ideas, but no one wants to talk. It appears they are afraid they'll be labeled as the "culprit."

a. Reflect what you consider the group members' feelings to be at that moment.

b. Call on each person for his/her ideas.

c. Wait a few moments. Someone will speak up, if only to break the silence.

Situation 3:

One of the group members openly criticizes the entire group. There is obvious defensiveness to the criticism.

a. Ask the group member why she or he is being so critical.

b. Change the subject diplomatically to reduce the defensiveness.

c. Ask the other group members how they feel about the criticism they've just received.

Situation 4:

Everyone in the meeting has expressed feelings and opinions about the reasons for low productivity. One of the members complains that she's tired of hearing how everyone "feels" and wants to see more progress in the meeting.

a. Move the discussion away from this sensitive area in order to reduce defensiveness in the group.

b. Ask the group members how they think they should proceed at this point.

c. Ask the group members for more factual information to support their opinions concerning low productivity.

Situation 5:

The group presents more opinions and factual data. One member is adamant about the cause of low productivity—a position you silently don't agree with. Group members ask for your opinion.

a. Ask the more adamant member to explain her position more fully.

b. Give the group members your own opinion and any additional information you feel might be helpful.

c. Summarize the situation up to now and ask for the group's input.

Situation 6:

One of the group members openly criticizes you for the narrow approach you have taken to identify a single cause for the problem of low productivity. He feels there may be more than one reason for the problem. The other group members are looking at you to see how you will react to their criticism.

    a. Defend your position. Remember you are the meeting leader.

    b. Communicate your reasoning again so the group understands the rationale for your approach.

    c. Have the group brainstorm possible causes and list them on a flip chart.

Situation 7:

After listing all the possible causes on a flip chart, the majority of the group agrees on the essential cause of the problem. You get a strong indication that they want to adjourn the meeting at this point.

    a. Devote a few minutes at this point to smoothing out some of the interpersonal conflicts which have occurred in the meeting.

    b. Remind the group the original purpose of the meeting was to develop a solution to the problem and decide on a course of action.

    c. Summarize the group's accomplishments thus far and ask for proposals to solve the problem to be submitted before the next morning.

Situation 8:

One of the members of the group has considerable experience and expertise and could be a valuable contributor to this meeting. However, she has not participated much because of some earlier criticism she received from another group member.

    a. Ask her what's bothering her.

b. Apologize to her concerning the earlier, unwarranted criticism.

c. Comment on her experience in this area and ask for her views.

Situation 9:

Two people have gotten into a personal argument. It's become pretty heated and the other members are sitting around the table observing and probably wondering what you intend to do about it.

a. You decide who is right after you've asked each man to restate his position.

b. Paraphrase each person's views, and ask an open question to the entire group, requesting them to give their views on the issue, and remind them to stay focused on the issue at hand.

c. Ask the two people to settle their argument later—after the meeting.

Situation 10:

The meeting has come to a standstill. The members are sharply divided over the best solution and it appears you've reached a stalemate.

a. You should now make the decision for the group.

b. Ask the members to choose a representative from each point of view to study the proposed solution.

c. Summarize the progress made thus far to stimulate thinking.

Situation 11:

You feel the group has come to some agreement concerning a specific course of action. You'd like the proposal to be acceptable to everyone and also get their commitment.

a. Check with each member to see if there is actually a consensus.

b. Assume the group members will accept the solution and ask for someone to volunteer.

c. Thank the group for their time and effort.

Situation12:

With a hand vote, everyone agrees on a specific course of action. Now you need to put it into action.

a. Assume someone will volunteer to develop a plan going forward.

b. Ask the group if there are any concerns.

c. Comment on the hard work the group put forth and assign responsibilities for the development of an implementation plan.

Recommended Answers

Situation	Behavior / Actions
1	C
2	A
3	C
4	C
5	B
6	C
7	B
8	C
9	B
10	C
11	A
12	C

References

Athanassiades, J.C. (June, 1973) *The Academy of Management Journal.* Vol. 16, No. 2 (June, 1973), pp. 207-226

Buckingham, M. & Coffman, C. (1999). *First, Break all the Rules: What the World's Greatest Managers do Differently.* New York: Simon & Schuster Publishing.

Collins, J. (2001). *Good to Great: Why Some Companies Make the Leap and Others Don't.* New York: Harper Collins Publishing.

Davis, K. (1967). *Human Relations at Work.* New York: McGraw-Hill Publishing.

Falcione, R.L. (1975). *Subordinate Satisfaction as a Function of Perceived Supervisor Credibility.* Paper presented at a meeting of the International Communication Association. Chicago, Illinois.

Falcione, R.L., J.C. McCroskey, & J.A. Daly. (1977). *Job Satisfaction as a Function of Employees' Communication Apprehension, Self-Esteem, and Perceptions of their Immediate Supervisors.* Paper presented at a meeting of the International Communication Association, Berlin, Germany.

Falcione, R.L. (1978). Subordinate Satisfaction as a Function of Communication Climate and Perceptions of Immediate Supervision. Paper presented at the Eastern Communication Association. Boston, Massachusetts.

Goldhaber, G., D. Porter, & M. Yates. *The ICA Communication Audit Survey Instrument: 1977 Organizational Norms.* Paper presented at a meeting of the International Communication Association, Berlin, Germany.

Goldhaber, G. (1979). *Organizational Communication.* Dubuque, Iowa: William C. Brown Publishing.

Leathers, D.B. (1976). *Nonverbal Communications Systems.* Boston: Allyn & Bacon Publishing.

Mehrabian, A. (1971). *Silent Messages.* Belmont, CA: Wadsworth Publishing.

Planty, E. & Machaver, W. (1952). *Upward Communications: A Project in Executive Development.*

Wagner, R. and Harter, J. (2006). *The 12 Elements of Great Managing.* New York: Gallup Press.

Whiteley, R.C. (1991). *The Customer-Driven Company.* New York: Addison-Wesley Publishing.

Whitely, R.C. and Hessan, D. (1996). *Customer-Centered Growth.* New York: Addison-Wesley Publishing.

About the Author

Ray Falcione combined a forty-five plus year career as President of Falcione Consulting Group (www.falcione.com) with that of professor of organizational communication, researcher/ author, and university administrator at the University of Maryland. Competencies in the area of conflict management, high performance teams, facilitation skills, coaching and mentoring skills, leadership and management development, quality improvement, communication audits, customer service, and briefing skills have led to a wide variety of consulting assignments. For over 25 years, a focus has been placed on Internet-based 360-degree feedback, using customized feedback instruments.

He has conducted organizational communication audits, and consulting services, including training in communication and leadership for numerous government organizations such as the General Accounting Office, various Maryland County Governments, Dept. of Agriculture, National Park Service, NOAA, HHS, NASA, and a US Senator's office. Other government clients include the U.S. Departments of the Air Force, Army, and Navy, Office of Personnel Management, and various Agencies in the Intelligence Community. Selected business clients in the private sector include eBay, the Mortgage Corporation, Investment Companies Institute, Lockheed-Martin, Boeing, IBM, AT&T, and Verizon.

He is a life member of the International Communication Association (ICA), past Vice President and Chairperson of the Organizational Communication Division of ICA, past President of the Metropolitan Washington Communication Association, and member of the Association for Talent Development (ATD).

Dr. Falcione holds a PhD in Organizational Communication from Kent State University. He has published and presented over sixty articles, papers, and book chapters in the United States, Europe and Asia, and has authored or co-authored eleven books dealing with research in organizational communication, published by Sage Publishing, and Scott-Foresman Publishing.

Made in the USA
Columbia, SC
22 December 2023

29260990R00117